GRINNELL'S GLACIER

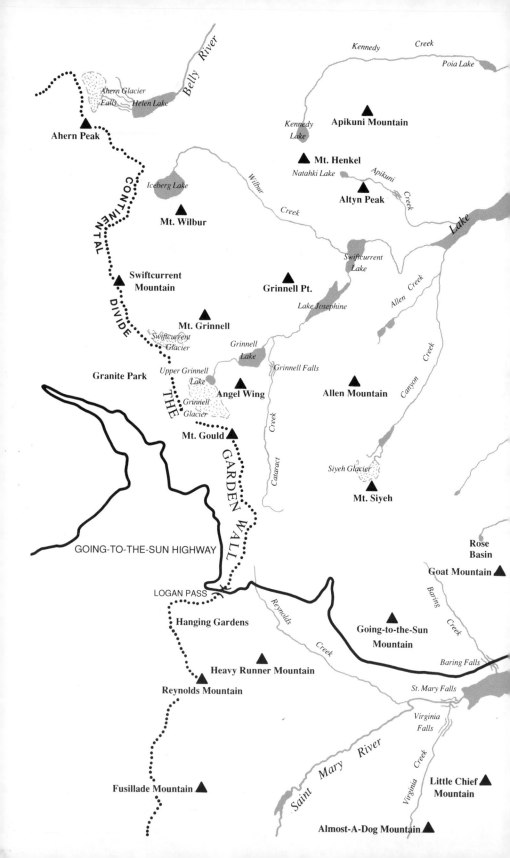

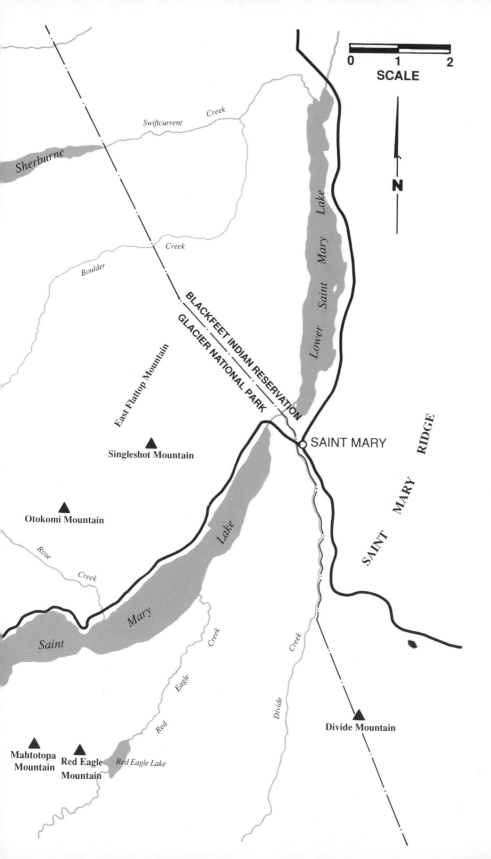

GRINNELL'S GLACIER

George Bird Grinnell
and Glacier National Park

Gerald A. Diettert

Foreword by Jerry De Santo

Mountain Press Publishing Company
Missoula, Montana

Copyright © 1992
Gerald A. Diettert

Map by Carla Majernik
Cover art and drawings by Dick Gravender

Library of Congress Cataloging-in-Publication Data

Diettert, Gerald A.
    Grinnell's glacier : George Bird Grinnell and the founding of
Glacier National Park / Gerald A. Diettert.
        p.   cm.
    Includes bibliographical references
    ISBN 0-87842-276-5 : $10.00
    1. Glacier National Park (Mont.)—History.   2. Grinnell, George
Bird, 1849-1938.   3. Naturalists—United States—Biography.
4. Conservationists—United States—Biography.   I. Title.
F737.G5D54   1992   92-4331
978.6'52—dc20   CIP

MOUNTAIN PRESS PUBLISHING COMPANY
2016 Strand Avenue • P.O. Box 2399
Missoula, Montana 59806 • (406) 728-1900

To my Mother and Father for giving me an interest in history,
To my Wife for encouraging my curiosity,
To my Professor for teaching me the ways.

Table of Contents

Foreword xi

About the Author.. xiii

Epigraph... xv

I: The Last Visit 1

II: The Out-Of-Doors Life 5

III: "To the Walled-In-Lakes," 1885..................................... 19

IV: "The Rock Climbers," 1887.. 35

V: "Slide Rock from Many Mountains," 1891 47

VI: The Ceded Strip, 1895 61

VII: "The Crown of the Continent" 73

VIII: An Uphill Push, 1906-1910 87

IX: Reluctant Hero... 97

Appendix A, Resolution of the Boone and Crockett Club 110

Appendix B, Books by George Bird Grinnell................................ 111

Sources and Notes 113

Bibliography... 119

Index... 125

Hiking to Grinnell Glacier, 1926.

Foreword

H. W. Fowler wrote that a foreword is distinguished from a preface when it is by "someone not the author." "Though arbitrary," he added, "the distinction is useful." With Fowler's tacit approval, the following comments are offered by someone not the author but a longtime admirer of both George Bird Grinnell and Glacier National Park.

George Bird Grinnell was a naturalist of the old school. A Ph.D. from Yale, his varied activities bear no resemblance to those of modern holders of the degree. Grinnell was trained in osteology (his dissertation was on the bone structure of the roadrunner) but very soon he branched out into ornithology, zoology and especially ethnography. Along the way, he became an ardent explorer and an avid hunter and fisherman. He was one of the truly great conservationists of the late nineteenth century and early twentieth century and was instrumental in founding the Audubon Society. Grinnell was associated with the magazine *Forest and Stream* (later, *Field and Stream*) for thirty-five years as a natural history editor, editor and president. His career as a writer and publisher led to the production of more than twenty books and hundreds of articles.

Grinnell first visited the area that was to become Glacier National Park in the fall of 1885. His earliest trips centered on the wild and mountainous St. Mary Lakes region. A few years later, he and his party worked their way to the head of the valley now called Many Glacier and to the glacier that soon came to be known as Grinnell Glacier. From his first trip, Grinnell was intrigued by the sight of Chief Mountain, rising in solitary splendor to the north.

In 1903 he climbed Chief, accompanied by Elizabeth (his bride of less than a year), Mr. and Mrs. John J. White, Jack Monroe and Billy Upham. Upham, the guide, had led Henry L. Stimson to the summit in 1892—the first ascent by a white man. The Grinnell party has been described as including the "first female ascent."

Beginning in 1905, Grinnell devoted much time and effort to the establishment of a national park to include the country he had roamed for twenty years. Finally, on May 11, 1910, President William Howard

Taft signed the bill creating Glacier National Park. Grinnell's greatest hope had become a reality.

In 1926 Grinnell made his last journey to Grinnell Glacier and Glacier National Park. Although seventy-six years old, he rode and walked to the glacier and stood upon it. His trips to the Glacier area had spanned forty-one years.

Of all the words of praise bestowed on George Bird Grinnell during his long and active life, the remarks of his old Glacier comrade, James Willard Schultz, may have pleased him the most. "He was one of the most indefatigable and daring mountain climbers that I have ever known.... No one could wish for a better camp companion. He was always ready to do his share of the work."

Grinnell often looked to the past and longed for the good old days. Incorrigibly melancholy, he wrote as early as 1886, of the "happy free life of olden time.... The mountain life of to-day is not the life of twenty, nor even of ten years ago.... I regret that changes that have come and others that I see near at hand." At a vigorous sixty-one years, he said, as did Macbeth, that he had "fallen into the sere and yellow leaf." He added that his "hold on the twig of life [was] already loosening." He lived on for another twenty-eight years.

In 1911 Grinnell traveled to the park to see it again "before it gets full of wagon roads and hotels." In 1913 he observed that the park "is now more or less full of tourists." What would he have thought of the 1,987,000 visitors who "saw" Glacier National Park, in 1990?

One hundred years have wrought changes to the Glacier country Grinnell knew. Though still wild, the park is cut here and there by roads and dotted by tourist-serving enclaves. Still haunting its wilderness are bighorn sheep, mountain goat and grizzly bear, as they did in Grinnell's day. The rivers and lakes still abound in fish. Adventuresome climbers come to Glacier Park to meet the challenge and seek the solace of the high peaks—as Grinnell did wholeheartedly so many years ago.

Modern visitors approaching the St. Mary valley from the south or east still see, as Grinnell did in 1885, one of the most spectacular alpine vistas in North America. The long view shows little change. To the northwest, Chief Mountain, Grinnell's "grand needle of rock," penetrates the sky from its isolated position. This was and is Grinnell country.

In 1926 President Calvin Coolidge told Grinnell: "The Glacier National Park is peculiarly your monument." Maurice Frink said it better in 1961: "He was there. He saw it happen. He was part of what he saw. And he wrote it all with clarity and honesty, with the scholar's precision and the pioneer's affection for a passing era."

Jerry DeSanto
Boundary Creek, Alberta

About the Author

Summer camping and hikes in Glacier National Park were a part of Gerald Diettert's childhood after the family moved to Missoula, Montana, where his father was a professor of botany. After completing medical school and specialty training, Diettert, with his wife, Ethel moved back to Missoula to raise three sons and a daughter, race sailboats and practice cardiology. Summers found the family camping at Rising Sun or Avalanche Creek campgrounds, hiking to Hidden Lake, Avalanche Basin or along the Garden Wall when the children were younger, advancing to trips over Siyeh or Piegan Pass as they got older.

He returned to the University of Montana in 1984, finishing a previously uncompleted B. A. degree at the same time his youngest son received his. Excited by a new exposure to the field of history, he obtained his M. A. in 1990.

Diettert is author of a number of medical articles, some nursing manuals and was editor of a medical journal for several years. This is his first non-medical book.

Recently retired, Diettert now has time to write, paint, golf, play with trains and hike with his wife to Grinnel Glacier.

"The steps which led to the establishment of the Glacier National Park have already been forgotten by most people. That, after all, is not important. The great thing is that this beautiful region has been saved for the public. . ."

—George Bird Grinnell, 1914

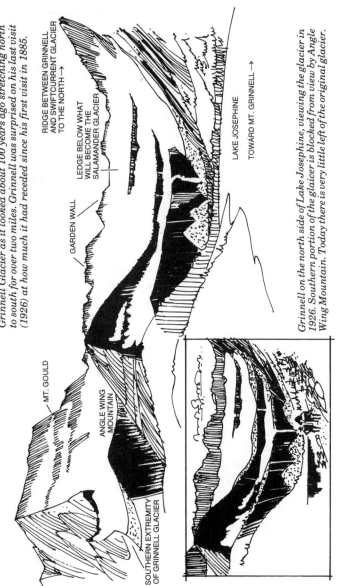

Grinnell Glacier as it looked about 100 years ago stretching north to south for over two miles. Grinnell was surprised on his last visit (1926) at how much it had receded since his first visit in 1885.

RIDGE BETWEEN GRINNELL AND SWIFTCURRENT GLACIER TO THE NORTH →

LEDGE BELOW WHAT WILL BECOME THE SALAMANDER GLACIER

GARDEN WALL

MT. GOULD

ANGLE WING MOUNTAIN

SOUTHERN EXTREMITY OF GRINNELL GLACIER

LAKE JOSEPHINE

TOWARD MT. GRINNELL →

Grinnell on the north side of Lake Josephine, viewing the glacier in 1926. Southern portion of the glacier is blocked from view by Angle Wing Mountain. Today there is very little left of the original glacier.

I

The Last Visit

EORGE BIRD GRINNELL and his wife, Elizabeth, arrived at Many Glacier Hotel without fanfare on July 11, 1926. Three years had passed since their last visit. The boys working as room clerks did not realize they were serving the namesake of the mountain just across the lake and a nearby glacier and they gave them a noisy room.

The next morning Morton J. Elrod, a biology professor from the University of Montana who spent summers working as a naturalist at Glacier National Park, recognized Grinnell in the lobby. The two men began talking and continued late into the evening. Grinnell remained anxious to visit "his glacier" once again, but feared his age of seventy-six might prevent him from making the climb. Elrod offered to accompany the older man, and he accepted.

Grinnell spent the next day riding along the base of "his mountain" on the north side of Lake Josephine and observed that the glacier was melting very fast. "All these glaciers are receding rapidly and after a time will disappear," he predicted. When he returned to the hotel, Elrod proposed they go to the glacier the next day. A small group of distinguished visitors also volunteered to travel with the two men. With typical self-effacement, Grinnell wondered in his diary: "Much talk about going there in my company. Why?"

In addition to Grinnell and Elrod, the party now included Margaret Kenney, daughter of Great Northern Railroad vice president W. P. Kenney; Mrs. A. J. Binder, wife of the manager of Many Glacier Hotel; and H. A. Noble, manager of the Glacier Park Company, and

1

his wife. Elizabeth Grinnell felt ill, as she often did when accompanying her husband in the mountains, so she remained at the hotel.

They started for the glacier about 11 A.M., traveling on horseback through the woods to the head of Lake Josephine. Then, after fording a stream on the old Kootenai Indian trail, they started up a series of steep switchbacks across the great red cliffs on the east face of Mount Grinnell, where, on a rocky shelf, the trail turned off to the west. After a stretch of relatively level, open travel, the party reached a small rushing stream, its cold waters cascading down the cliffs to turquoise Grinnell Lake far below. Protruding rock ledges made the last leg of the trail too narrow for horses, so the party had to complete the trip on foot.

They stopped for lunch beside a small stream in a tiny valley bordered by a grove of stunted subalpine fir. Across the stream, the rubble of the glacier's lateral moraine rose abruptly on its north side. Refreshed after their rest, they climbed over the moraine and up onto the slush-covered surface of the glacier. Elrod asked Hans Riess, a Swiss guide who had just finished leading a party of twenty over the glacier, to escort them; he roped together all but Elrod. As they wandered over the ice, Grinnell noted great changes since his first visit to the glacier in 1887, thirty-nine years earlier. He remembered ice extending more than 100 feet higher to the top of the northern lateral moraine and against the face of the mountain to the top of the

George Bird Grinnell visits Grinnell Glacier for the last time, 1926.
—Elrod collection, University of Montana, Mansfield Library

Garden Wall; below, it reached almost to the edge of the ledge where Grinnell had once killed a huge ram sheep. Even the ice caves where he and Elizabeth were photographed three years before had disappeared. Their exploration completed, the party climbed down the moraine to the trail. "Leg weary," Grinnell fell twice. "Everyone was sympathetic about my progress," he wrote that evening in his diary. He felt stronger after resting a half hour and drinking some coffee. He mounted his horse and "trotted all the way back," reaching the hotel about 9 P.M.

Earlier, while standing on "his glacier," Grinnell looked east across the valley of the Swiftcurrent; Apikuni Mountain rose from behind the bulk of Mount Henkel; Allen Mountain guarded the southern flank of the valley. To his right stood massive Mount Gould and its shoulder, Mount Monroe. On his left, Mounts Wilbur and Grinnell—"my mountain"—filled his view. In the wake of this visit to the glacier, Grinnell surely thought—as he had forty years earlier when he wrote these words—of those who had shared the outdoor life with him:

> I see pass before me, as in a vision, the forms and faces of grave, silent men, whom once I called my friends. They have fired their last shot, they have kindled their last camp-fire, they have gone over the Range, crossed the great Divide. There were giants in those days, and of that heroic race how few are left alive! Lingering illness, the storms of winter, the pistol ball of the white man, the rifle shot of the savage, have sadly thinned their ranks. And none have risen, nor can arise, to fill places left vacant. The conditions which made these men what they were no longer exist.[1]

Grinnell and friend digging fossils with the Marsh expedition in 1870 in northwest Nebraska. Major North and Pawnee scouts offer protection from hostile Sioux and Cheyenne.

II

The Out-Of-Doors Life

G EORGE BIRD GRINNELL'S exposure to the fascinating world out-of-doors began early in his childhood. In 1853 at the age of four, while still living in his birthplace of Brooklyn, he became enchanted with his uncle Tom. Twenty-year-old Thomas P. Grinnell had come to New York from Greenfield, Massachusetts, and lived with George's family while working in a dry goods store.

Uncle Tom readily seized his young nephew's imagination with stories of hunting and fishing, and he brought his tales to life with pictures of birds. A large collection of mounted birds and mammals delighted the youngster whenever he visited his uncle's family home in Greenfield. In an autobiographical manuscript entitled "Memories" Grinnell wrote for his own nieces and nephews many years later, he recalled, ". . . up to the time when I was twelve or fifteen years of age, I had no pleasanter hours when at Greenfield, than those spent among Uncle Tom's birds in what was called the 'bird room.'"

When Grinnell was seven his family moved to Audubon Park, an area along the Hudson River between Manhatten's future 155th and 158th streets. Naturalist John James Audubon, who had died about six years earlier, had built homes in the park for himself and his two sons, Victor Gifford and John Woodhouse, plus several for rent.

In this sylvan setting young Grinnell went killifishing and crabbing in a nearby tidal pond as well as skinny-dipping, to the embarrassment of passengers on the Hudson River trains. He caught bats in a nearby barn and stalked robins and wild pigeons with the hickory bow and arrows cousin George Bird bought for him from the Indians at Saratoga. The countryside stirred the imaginations of George and

5

his younger brothers; three-year-old Frank "made an Indian" of two-year-old Mort by stripping him "stark naked in the chilly breeze" while George disrobed down to his shorts and stuck plumes from a feather duster in a handkerchief tied around his head.

The Grinnell children and others in the neighborhood attended a school conducted by Madame Audubon in her bedroom on the second floor of Victor's home. The walls in both Audubon brothers' houses were filled with mementos from their naturalist father: antlers of deer and elk supported rifles and shotguns, paintings of birds and animals, and trophies from the Missouri River, "a region," Grinnell later wrote, "which in those days seemed infinitely remote and romantic with its tales of trappers, trading posts and Indians." In addition to bats, the barn near the house held "great stacks of the old red, muslin-bound ornithological biographies and boxes of bird skins collected by the

Victor Gifford Audubon House.

6

naturalist." John Woodhouse Audubon, who continued his father's work, frequently received boxes of fresh specimens that fascinated the boys as they gathered around "to wonder at the strange animals that were revealed."

Grinnell began hunting secretly with a neighbor boy when he was eleven or twelve. From the village tailor they borrowed an old military musket "taller than either boy, and . . . so heavy that unaided neither could hold it to the shoulder." After buying powder and shot at the town store, they sneaked off to the woods and aimed at small birds and rabbits. The station agent at 152d Street sometimes loaned them a single-barreled shotgun that they used with "great joy and success."

Uncle William Grinnell, upon learning of the boys' excursions, presented George with a light, double-barreled gun that he used with his parents' consent to bag quail, English snipe, cottontail rabbits and an occasional duck. This gun provided the impetus for his first camping trip, across the river to the Palisades. The boys slept on the ground and ate cold food, since neither knew how to build a fire; adding to this discomfort, during the night rain filled the barrels of the shotgun propped against a tree.

Upon Grinnell's graduation from "Grandma" Audubon's school, his parents sent him to the nearby French institute to complete his grammar schooling. In 1863, as preparation for college, he enrolled in a three-year program at the Churchill Military School at Sing Sing (now Ossining). Grinnell was not interested in college, but his father adamantly insisted that he attend Yale, the alma mater of several ancestors. His teachers warned that he would not pass Yale's entrance exam, so George spent all summer studying Latin and Greek; he passed the test with conditions in Greek and geometry.

Little interested in academics, George found himself "perpetually in trouble." Hazing and hat-stealing occupied much of his time. In a demonstration of athletic prowess, he climbed the lightning rod on the tower of the Lyceum one stormy night and inscribed the numbers of his class year on the clock face with red paint. It remained for several days, to the pride of his class, until the college carpenter could devise a way to reach and remove the graffiti. Caught hazing a freshman, Grinnell was suspended from school for a year and was sent to Connecticut for tutoring. Unengaged, he spent most of his time outdoors, taking long walks, rowing on the river, and tramping over the fields on moonlit nights. He failed his exams, but studied diligently through spring vacation and managed to reenter Yale, finally graduating in 1870.

House of John Woodhouse Audubon.

Westward Bound

Toward the end of his senior year Grinnell heard that Professor
Othniel C. Marsh planned to conduct a fossil-collecting expedition in
the West. Inspired by Capt. Mayne Reid's travel writings from the
plains and the mountains during the 1840s and eager to visit such
places himself, Grinnell volunteered to assist Marsh. The professor
hesitated at first, then reluctantly accepted his offer and asked him to

8

recommend other possible members. Grinnell suggested several friends, all of whom Marsh approved.

The party left New Haven on June 30, 1870, then spent several days in Omaha shooting their new rifles for the first time before traveling on to Fort McPherson. On their first day out they met Buffalo Bill Cody returning from an investigation of a Cheyenne Indian attack. Maj. Frank North and two Pawnee scouts accompanied the fossil hunters to protect them from hostiles. They crossed the torrid Sand Hills and Dismal River to the Loup Fork, where they collected fossils of prehistoric horses, miniature camels and a mastodon. On their next outing, near Fort D. A. Russell in Wyoming, Grinnell and a friend became separated from the main party for two days without provisions. They encountered a prairie fire and briefly thought they were under Indian attack during the night when one of the horses pulled a picket pin.

The expedition made spectacular fossil finds: ancient turtles, rhinoceri, giant sea serpents, the wing finger of a pterodactyl, the four-foot jaw bone of a giant horned Titanothere and the exotic remains of an oreodon, which Grinnell described as "a remarkable animal combining characteristics of the modern sheep, pig and deer." Grinnell saw his first live elk, but did not get a chance to shoot at one.

Moving on to Fort Bridger, the Marsh party found dinosaur fossils in Tertiary lake-bed formations at the edge of the Uinta Mountains. Grinnell experienced a taste of Indian life when he spent a few nights in the skin lodge of some trappers: ". . . the existence of these families seemed to me to be absolutely ideal. I desired enormously to spend the rest of my life with these people." Instead, he remained with the party and went on to Salt Lake City, where he and the rest of the students met Brigham Young and admired his twenty-two daughters. A visit to San Francisco, Yosemite and "the Big Trees" completed the trip. Triumphantly, the expedition returned to New Haven with thirty-five boxes of fossils for the Peabody Museum; Grinnell arrived home in time for Thanksgiving dinner.

Grinnell's father, principal broker for Commodore Cornelius Vanderbilt, expected his son eventually to take his place in the large and profitable business. Shortly after returning home George entered the office as an unpaid clerk. Yet he maintained a deep interest in science and scoured the menageries and taxidermy shops for fossils and unusual birds. He often spent evenings skinning and stuffing specimens in his basement workshop.

By the summer of 1872 Grinnell yearned to visit the West again. Since Major North could not accompany him, his brother, Capt. Luther North, agreed to take out a small party. Captain North met

Grinnell at the Union Pacific's Elk Creek station and they hurried south to overtake the Pawnee tribe, which had left several weeks earlier to hunt buffalo. After joining the Indian camp near the Republican River, the newcomers participated in an attack on a herd by about 800 men, most armed only with bows and arrows. This event, which Grinnell described in "A Summer Hunt," published as a chapter in *Pawnee Hero Stories and Folk Tales*, marked the beginning of his lifelong interest in American Indians; he also found an enduring friend in "Lute" North.

The following summer Grinnell again returned to Nebraska and later wrote, "Though I had been West two seasons, I had never shot

Prof. O. C. Marsh and members of his expedition in the field near Fort Bridger, Wyoming. Standing (left to right): Dr. Thomas Carter, J. W. Griswold, H. B. Sargent, G. B. Grinnell, C. W. Betts, O. C. Marsh, C. T. Ballard, J. R. Nicholson, J. M. Russell. Sitting: Eli Whitney, A. H. Ewing, H. Ziegler, and Bill, the cook.

at an elk, and like all boys, I was eager to do so." He joined Luther North at Columbus and together they hunted elk on the Cedar River and at the junction of the Loup and Platte.[2]

Upon Grinnell's return home in early September, his father retired, turning the business over to his son. Three weeks later the Panic of 1873 struck without warning. Facing several bankruptcy suits, the business would have collapsed had not the senior Grinnell returned from his brief retirement and supplied both money and influence. To escape his family's worries, young Grinnell began writing short hunting stories for a newly established sporting newspaper, *Forest and Stream*. It published his first article, describing his recent elk hunt in Nebraska, in the October issue under the pseudonym of "Ornis."

By spring of 1874, Grinnell's father had stabilized the business and retired again. Without his father to keep him there, and possessing a "settled dislike for the business," Grinnell dissolved the firm and went back to New Haven to volunteer at the Peabody Museum as an assistant to Marsh. He had barely settled in his new quarters when Gen. Philip H. Sheridan invited Marsh to collect fossils on a summer expedition to the Black Hills of the Teton Sioux, "then an unknown and mysterious region." Marsh passed the invitation on to Grinnell, who accepted it without hesitation. He asked Luther North to join him, and they traveled to St. Paul, where they received orders from Col. William Ludlow, chief engineer of the Department of Dakota. Previously, in New York City, Grinnell had met James G. Blaine and Lt. Col. George A. Custer at the old Fifth Avenue Hotel. Now, on the train to Bismarck, he met the colonel again, this time with his wife. At Fort Abraham Lincoln, across the river from Bismarck, Grinnell became acquainted with the officers of the Seventh Cavalry and the celebrated scout, "Lonesome" Charley Reynolds.

During the three weeks before the expedition departed, Grinnell collected birds along the Missouri River and the adjacent high prairie. He also dined at Custer's house and listened to his host's hunting exploits, socialized with officers in the billiards room, and made expedition plans with the other scientists.

On July 2, 1874, sixteen musicians on white horses played "The Girl I Left Behind Me" as the command moved out, heading west and south for the two-month reconnaissance. Custer, "a man of great energy," ordered reveille at 4 A.M., breakfast at 4:30, and the command to march at 5. The scientists rode with Custer and the headquarters, followed a half mile behind by the cavalry, then the wagons and the beef herd, and finally the infantry units. The Indian scouts ranged far ahead on both flanks. Grinnell noted the country was full of game;

"antelope were everywhere in extraordinary numbers." At one point he took a shot that must have astonished even Custer:

> I saw immediately before me, and perhaps 75 yards distant, a buck antelope, at which—without very much thought—I fired, and the antelope fell. On going up to it, I discovered its four legs were broken, and then examined it with some care. The ball had entered the left side, just back of the shoulder, and . . . chipped a peice of bone out of the olecranon, or point of the elbow. It had gone through the animal's body, broken the right humerus, turned at right angles, . . . broken the right femur, turned again at right angles, and struck the left hock of the antelope so severe a blow that it had unjointed the hock. . . . Close to the animal's hind legs I picked up the rifle ball, flattened out to the size of a half dollar, quite circular, but, of course, thicker in the middle than at the edges.[3]

Grinnell and North, on a couple of "old condemned cavalry horses," arrived in camp daily with fresh venison. Only once, where the lush mountains gave way to dry plains and badlands near the Belle Fourche River, did the pair search for fossils. During a three-day ride up and down the steep ravines, their horses near death and their supplies exhausted, they found a part of the lower jaw of a rhinoceros. As the command began its return march, Colonel Ludlow asked Grinnell to write a report on the birds and mammals of the region. Ludlow and Lt. Fred D. Grant, Custer's aide and son of the president, argued about who should receive it; Grinnell submitted the completed paper to Ludlow.

Grinnell's report must have impressed Colonel Ludlow; he asked Grinnell to serve as naturalist with him on a reconnaissance in Montana the following spring. Marsh approved, and Grinnell recruited his friend, Yale instructor E. S. Dana, to accompany him as geologist. The two men met Ludlow in St. Paul and then traveled by rail to Bismarck, where Ludlow hired Charley Reynolds as their scout. The steamer *Josephine* took the party upriver to Carroll, Montana, a small settlement of two trading stores and a half dozen cabins on the eastern edge of the Judith Basin.

While waiting for Ludlow, who was delayed by his brother's illness, Dana and Grinnell hunted, discovered some fossils, and met the famed fur trapper "Liver Eating" Johnson. Since supplies started running low, the party decided to move on to Camp Baker. Ludlow and his brother arrived in Carroll on the next boat, and, finding no horses, had to walk to Camp Baker. "It is better to imagine rather than to describe the language which they used during this walk," Grinnell noted later in his "Memories." Ludlow finally caught up with his command at Fort Ellis.

The expedition moved on to Yellowstone National Park, where Grinnell observed the region's natural wonders as well as wanton destruction of animals solely for their hides. His report on the birds and mammals there remains pertinent; far more significant, though, was his letter to Ludlow that accompanied the report and marked the beginning of his long career as a conservationist:

> It may not be out of place here to call your attention to the terrible destruction of large game, for their hides alone, which is constantly going on in . . . Montana and Wyoming. . . . Buffalo, elk, mule-deer, and antelope are being slaughtered by thousands each year, without regard to age or sex, and at all seasons. . . . Females of all species are as eagerly pursued in the spring, when just about to bring forth their young, as at any other time. It is estimated that during the winter of 1874-75 not less than 3,000 elk were killed for their hides alone. . . . Buffalo and mule-deer suffer even more severely than the elk, and antelope nearly as much. . . . It is certain that, unless in some way the destruction of these animals can be checked, the large game still so abundant in some localities will ere long be exterminated.[4]

In May 1876 Grinnell received a telegram from Colonel Custer asking him to be his guest on an expedition up the Yellowstone toward the Big Horn Mountains. Fortunately, the museum was busy with new materials, and Marsh thought there would be no opportunity to collect fossils or even search for new sites on a military expedition, so he refused to let Grinnell go. Grinnell was shooting woodcock at his father's summer place in Milford, Connecticut, when he heard the news from the Little Big Horn. He wrote in his "Memories":

> Had I gone with Custer I should have in all probability been mixed up in the Custer battle, for I should have been either with Custer's command, or with that of Reno, and would have been right on the ground when the Seventh Cavalry was wiped out. Very likely I should have been with Reno's command as Charley Reynolds and I were close friends and commonly rode together.

Forest and Stream

That spring, *Forest and Stream* editor Charles Hallock fired his natural history editor and asked Grinnell to take the position. He accepted, happy to work for $10 a week. The two men sent materials back and forth through the mail; in addition to editing, Grinnell wrote book reviews and a page or two of copy each week. Confident in the future of the sporting journal, he began buying stock in *Forest and Stream*.

In the summer of 1877 Grinnell traveled to western Nebraska, where Frank North and Buffalo Bill Cody had established a ranch to run Texas longhorns on the source of the Dismal River. The ranch, "a couple of tents stuck up on the edge of the alkaline lake," disappointed Grinnell, but game was plentiful. During his return home he developed fever, chills and delirium, and barely survived the trip. He spent the next seven weeks in bed recuperating.

> For a good part of that time I was always out of my head at night, and my delirium always took one form. I imagined myself riding about the cattle, saw great banks of clouds coming up in the west with thunder and lightning, and then the cattle would break away, and, of course, we would all ride after them as hard as we could.[5]

The next summer Grinnell and William H. Reed, future curator of the museum at the University of Wyoming, explored the Jurassic exposures in the Como Bluffs near Medicine Bow, Wyoming. Grinnell's brother Mort joined them later and they stayed at the railroad station, "shooting ducks during the day, sleeping on the floor of the station at night, and . . . having a very good time." He stopped at the North ranch on his way home and found they had replaced the tents with "a fine sod house."

Grinnell hunted in North Park, Colorado, in the summer of 1879 and found deer, elk, mountain sheep and bear in abundance. He wrote about this trip, using the pseudonym "Yo" for the first time, in a nine-part series in the September and October issues of *Forest and Stream*. His reflections on the trip later formed the basis for *Jack the Young Trapper*, one of his series of books for boys.

Over the years, Grinnell's stock in *Forest and Stream* increased, and by 1880 he owned almost one-third of the enterprise; his father also had invested in it. Edward R. Wilbur, the treasurer, discussed the affairs of the newspaper from time to time with Grinnell and finally asked him to take over as president and editor because Hallock's drinking made him increasingly erratic. The Grinnells' stock combined with Wilbur's gave them control of the company and they forced Hallock out. Grinnell, due to receive his Ph.D. in osteology and vertebrate paleontology from Yale that year, resigned his position at the Peabody Museum and returned to New York to assume his new responsibilities.

Grinnell quickly organized a competent staff, with Charles B. Reynolds as managing editor, Fred Mather on fishing, C. P. Kunhardt on yachting, Franklin Satterthwaite on dogs, and Josiah Whitley on hunting. T. C. Banks served as secretary, Wilbur as treasurer, and John Banks as the bookkeeper and cashier. "We printed a good paper, had a large circulation, and began almost at once to make plenty of money."6

Grinnell's new duties as president of Forest and Stream Publishing Company and editor of *Forest and Stream* prevented him from traveling West again until the summer of 1881. A. H. Barney, president of the Northern Pacific Railroad, invited him to travel across the West that year on the northern line. The eastern part of the Northern Pacific, by 1881, had reached eastern Montana; its Pacific Northwest tracks formed a triangle between Portland, Seattle, and Spokane. Reaching the western end of the line in Portland was an adventure in itself. First Grinnell, Dana and another friend, E. H. Landon, took the Union Pacific to San Francisco, then caught a coastal steamer north to Vancouver Island.

At Victoria, British Columbia, Grinnell met two sportsmen who had contributed articles to *Forest and Stream* and they took him hunting for deer and bear. He saw his first mountain goat at Burrard Inlet and chronicled his trip in *Forest and Stream*. Later he drew from his experiences on this trip when he wrote *Jack, The Young Canoeman*. Finally Grinnell and his two friends arrived in Portland and began their return trip, traveling on the Northern Pacific to the village of Spokane. From there they journeyed east on wagons and stage-coaches through Pend d'Oreille, "Jaco," Missoula and Deer Lodge to Silver Bow, where they embarked on the narrow gauge railroad to Corrine, Utah, and returned to New York on the Union Pacific.

By 1881 the eastern section of the Northern Pacific Railroad reached Yellowstone National Park, making the region readily accessible to the public. Privately, the railroad organized the Yellowstone Park Improvement Company and obtained from the assistant secretary of the interior ten leases of 640 acres, each at prominent points of interest and natural wonders in the park. As a first step, the company erected a sawmill to cut timber for the construction of hotels. Grinnell, through *Forest and Stream*, opposed these efforts to monopolize public property for private gain. In 1882 he initiated a campaign to maintain the integrity of the park by enforceable laws and regulations. Over the years, largely through his efforts, the Lacey Act passed Congress in 1894, finally providing regulations for Yellowstone and future national parks.

In August 1882 Grinnell returned to Como, Wyoming, and hunted elk with William Reed in the Shirley Basin. Although antelope were plentiful, elk were scarce, so the men spent several of their hunting days prospecting. They filed fourteen mining claims in quartz ledges, some with "queer yellowish green crystals," as Grinnell described them in his diary. Assays of the various claims showed traces of white iron, silver and copper.

The next spring Grinnell purchased a 1,100-acre ranch in the Shirley Basin and hired Reed to run it. The ranch soon fell into economic hardship; during the first winter, one-third of its 3,000 sheep died. The following summer Grinnell sold the surviving sheep and restocked the operation with cattle and horses. But the terrible "winter of blue snow" in 1886-87 wiped out most of his livestock. After Reed left the ranch in 1888 Grinnell leased it out, often calling upon Luther North to find tenants and handle the arrangements. He finally sold the ranch in 1903, after fifteen years of struggle, declaring the project a "financial failure."

In October 1880 *Forest and Stream* published the first of many articles by James Willard Schultz. "Hunting in Montana" described a hunting trip on the upper Marias River. Schultz, a rebel since childhood, had come to Montana in 1877 at the age of seventeen and worked for Joseph Kipp at his Fort Conrad trading post. Within a few years he married a fifteen-year-old Piegan girl and received a Piegan name, *Apikuni*, meaning White (Buffalo) Robe. Schultz adopted the Piegan way of life and even participated in raids on other tribes. He continued to write about hunting trips and Indian anecdotes, and *Forest and Stream* printed many of Schultz's articles through the mid-1880s.[7]

One account, "To The Chief Mountain," published in December 1885, fired Grinnell's imagination. Printed after Grinnell had already returned from a trip to this "little known section of the Rocky Mountains just south of the international boundary line in northwestern Montana," the article described hunting bighorn sheep and mountain goats and catching twelve-pound trout in lakes "walled in by stupendous mountains . . . peak after peak of jagged mountains, some of them with sheer cliffs thousands of feet high." Schultz also mentioned a glacier: "Beyond the head of the lake is a long, wide, densely timbered valley, and on the upper left-hand side of this valley is a mountain, the top of which is a true glacier . . . at least 300 feet thick. We could see large fissures in it. . . ."

Grinnell left New York City in August 1885 to see these walled-in lakes for himself. After a week's pause in Yellowstone, he took the Northern Pacific to Helena, where he caught the mail stage and rode 116 miles farther to Fort Benton. Apikuni would be waiting for him there with a wagon.

BEAR WOMAN   RED EAGLE   JAMES WILLARD SCHULTZ   GEORGE BIRD GRINNELL   JOSEPH KIPP

Bear Pipe Ceremony.

III

"To the Walled-In Lakes," 1885

T HE SLENDER YOUNG MAN dressed in well-worn camp clothes stepped down from the mail stage carrying his canvas-covered bedroll, "war sack," Sharps .45-caliber rifle and split-bamboo fly rod. Clearly George Bird Grinnell was no tenderfoot, and his guide, James Willard Schultz—"Apikuni"—was not surprised to learn that Grinnell owned a Wyoming ranch and had been with Custer in the Black Hills. The two men set out at once from Fort Benton on the ninety-mile trip to the Blackfeet Agency on Badger Creek, arriving there August 30, 1885. Grinnell paternalistically spent the next day visiting Indian children at the two local schools.

On September 1, Charles Rose, a twenty-eight-year-old mixed blood more commonly known as Yellowfish or *Otokomi*, joined Grinnell and Apikuni. His father was Albert Rose, an American Fur Company employee who helped build Fort Benton. His mother was *Ahkai Sinahki*, the full-blooded Blackfoot daughter of Running Crane, a Piegan chief who had given his Indian name, *Apikuni*, to Schultz.

The three men left on their journey to the lakes walled in by mountains beyond the St. Mary lakes. Their wagon carried a ten-foot-square wall tent, a sheet iron cook stove, bedding, provisions and a fourteen-foot skiff. Each man carried a rifle, and Apikuni also brought a shotgun. For the first forty-five miles, they followed a remnant of the Old North Trail. At Cut Bank Creek they secured two saddle horses—an old, tough but steady buffalo horse named Jerry for Grinnell and a spirited little blue for Apikuni. After unhitching the team and putting them out for the night, Grinnell set up his fly rod and caught half a dozen trout, each under a pound, "and, as is so

19

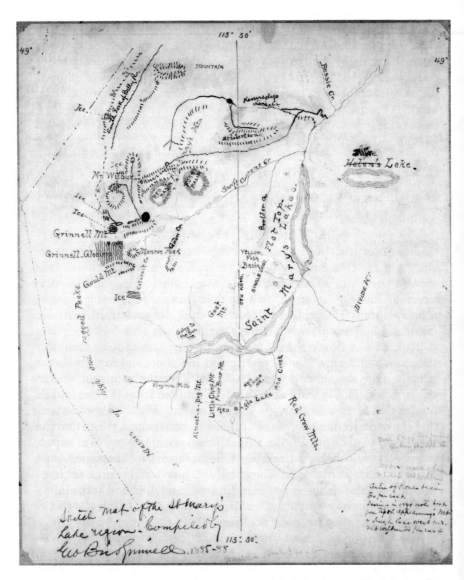

Sketch map of St. Mary's Lake region compiled by George Bird Grinnell, 1885-88. —Glacier National Park Archives

20

often the case with fisherman, lost one which we imagined was larger than all the rest." Just before sunset the clouds lifted, giving them a glimpse of Chief Mountain, impressive though still seventy miles away.[8]

Grinnell noted an "utter dearth of large game" because of the heavy hunting by the Piegans during the Starvation Winter of 1883-84. ". . . Even the jack rabbits and cotton-tails seem to have all been killed off, and there is hardly a prairie dog or a ground squirrel to be seen." They headed west toward the Milk River Ridge, where they discovered great numbers of ducks in the swampy areas of the flat bottom. A violent rainstorm hit as they traveled along a tributary of the Milk River's south fork, drenching them before they set up camp in an alder thicket. Yellowfish entertained Grinnell and Apikuni during the evening with Blackfoot stories. As they settled into their bedrolls, Grinnell noticed "the rain had turned into snow, which was coming down softly and slowly, melting as it fell."

The next morning they climbed St. Mary Ridge. For the first time Grinnell saw the valley of the St. Mary lakes. Through the changing clouds of mist he made out "the stern black faces of tremendous escarpments which rose from the water's very edge. . . . The occasional gleam of permanent snow far down the mountain sides hint at a glacial origin for the lakes." Grinnell recalled that Apikuni had seen glaciers when he visited this place the previous year.

The snow-covered ground made their steep descent to the lower lake more difficult. The men wrapped log chains around the rear wheels of the wagon for traction. Apikuni drove the team and worked the brake while Grinnell and Yellowfish pulled from the two saddle horses tied behind to keep the wagon straight. Rather than controlling the descent, the log chains acted like runners on a sleigh and the wagon skidded downhill. They finally edged it into a grove of aspen, then cut a path to the bottom, and from there drove alongside Lower St. Mary Lake to its head. They pitched their tent in an open, level meadow of knee-deep grass. After dinner Grinnell fished at the lake's inlet and caught a small whitefish, but "the great fish lying on the bottom . . . paid no heed" to his flies.

For the next two days, Grinnell and Yellowfish hunted unsuccessfully north of the upper lake on the mountain Apikuni had named East Flattop the year before. Above the tree line a "keen wind . . . and drenching fog . . . penetrated to one's very marrow." Yellowfish's toes protruded from his torn moccasins; Grinnell was soaked to his knees. In the *Forest and Stream* article, he wrote:

> The life of a sheep hunter is not one of luxurious ease. He must breast the steepest ascents, and must seek for his game over

ridges , along precipices and up peaks, and follow it to its home among the clouds. . . . The sheep hunter must have good lungs, tough muscles, a clear head and an iron nerve if he wishes to be successful in this difficult pursuit. Sheep hunting is no boy's play, and in these mountains it calls forth all a man's physical powers. . . . Nowadays the man who kills a sheep usually earns it several times over before he gets the meat to camp.

The climbing was slow and difficult, especially on the talus slopes. In some places they crossed large, sharp cubes of rock; in others, banks of loose shale moved under their feet. Even though sign was abundant in the barren landscape, they saw no sheep. Discouraged, the two men turned toward camp. Grinnell was "glad enough after saddling up to clamber on to old Jerry and ride him down, even over the worst and steepest parts of the trail."

Stiff and sore the next day, Grinnell decided to "just loaf about camp all day long." By late morning, he grew restless: "In theory, loafing is a most delightful way of passing the time, but in practice it fails to satisfy." He decided to fish again at the inlet while Apikuni shot a few widgeons to supplement their dwindling provisions.

Hunting Sheep

A horseman appeared on a distant ridge, then rode towards them. He was a Kootenai from a camp several miles downriver. Though the Kootenais primarily trapped beaver, they hunted to supply their camp. Despite the scarcity of local game, they had recently killed forty sheep, a few elk, a black bear, a grizzly and a moose. Two years had passed since they had seen and killed any buffalo, their traditional food. The sheep, they reported, were high up among the rocks and hard to reach. Grinnell visited their camp and found the party had just killed four more sheep, "the meat of which now hung from their saddles. The news of their success filled [him] with rage and envy." He arranged for a Kootenai to guide his hunt the next morning.

At 10 A.M., two "well grown boys" rode into Grinnell's camp. It started to rain as he and Yellowfish saddled their horses and followed the guides. With "blankets flapping and quirts flying," the two youths took "mischievous pleasure" in riding their mounts without mercy. After a steep climb, they left the horses at the timber's edge and struggled up the slippery grass slope to a level spot. Grinnell later wrote:

> At our feet the plateau ended, the ground dropped off sharply for a hundred feet, and a deep naked saddle extended from the spur on which we stood to the main mountain, which had all the

boldness and ruggedness characteristic of the range in this region. On the west the saddle broke off sharply in a very steep clay slope, and to the east by a more gentle descent into a deep ravine, in which grew a thick mat of stunted spruces, among which were the fallen and decaying trunks of some very large trees. Above the saddle for perhaps 1,000 feet was the gray talus slope, rocks piled on rocks in wild confusion, just as the fragments had fallen from the heights above. The slope seemed too steep for ascent, but faintly lined upon it in all directions could be discerned the sheep trails leading up and down.

A fierce rainstorm suddenly arrived "with showers of cold rain and squalls of snow, and clouds of chilling mist" assaulting the hunters on the bare mountainside. They found refuge behind a huge rock, then decided to send the older Indian boy to the east end of the rocky wall to drive game toward the rest of the party. While Grinnell shared his pipe with the younger Kootenai, Yellowfish built a fire down in the ravine. The older Kootenai soon returned, reporting snow and fog on the other side of the mountain too heavy to reveal any sheep. Cold and wet, the hunters returned to camp. Yellowfish suggested to Grinnell that, if this hunt proved successful, upon his return to the agency he should offer a Bear Pipe dance with a medicine pipe sacred to the Sun and other gods.

Grinnell returned to the same mountain the next day with two different Kootenais. Once they had tied the horses and begun the ascent on foot, Grinnell found he was a poor climber compared to the Indians. Out of breath, he had to stop to rest. He tried to tell his companions to slow down using sign language, but they did not understand and soon left him far behind, finally disappearing over the bench.

"It began to blow and snow furiously" when Grinnell heard three shots up the canyon and then saw a sheep's head peer from behind a ridge 300 yards away. Alarmed by the gunfire, the animal tried to pass above him behind a rock wall; suddenly it stopped between two rocks 150 yards away, with only its head and neck visible. Through the blinding flakes of the snow squall the hunter fired and saw the sheep bound wildly before bolting headlong down the mountain; he had no chance for a second shot. Leaping from rock to rock, excited by the action, Grinnell followed the footprints and tiny drops of blood down the loose shale slope and later wrote:

> There is something rather horrible in the wild and savage excitement that one feels under such circumstances as these; the mingling of exultation over the apparently successful pursuit, tempered by the doubt about securing the prey, and then the

fierce delight . . . when the capture is assured. These feelings seem to be those which the wolf must have when he is pulling down the exhausted deer, or the hound when the tired fox pants along just ahead of him, and the fierce triumph of success is heard in his exultant mellow bay. It seems shocking that a respectable civilized and well-ordered being . . . should . . . indulge in such brutal feelings. It shows how thin is the veneer of civilization which hides the brute in our nature and how easily this veneer is rubbed off, showing underneath it the character of the animal.

The yearling ewe lay dead below a twelve foot ledge, its windpipe and principal artery in the neck severed by the rifle ball—a lucky shot. Dressed out, the sheep weighed about ninety pounds. Since the Indians had not returned, Grinnell faced the task of carrying the meat by himself to the horses three miles away. "Now I am a little man," he wrote, "slight, and rather feeble than athletic, and usually find my own weight quite enough to carry." Nevertheless, he lifted the load to his back, slung his rifle in front, and started up the hill, stopping every few feet to get his breath. He fell once, which made him mad; he shouldered the carcass and rested four times before reaching the top of the long, steep hill. After sighting the horses, he dragged it the rest of the way and loaded it onto his mount, finishing just as the Indians arrived, each carrying half a sheep that they had shot. Still disgruntled at having to carry a whole sheep alone, Grinnell amused himself by guiding the Indians back to camp along the trail he had used the day before.

That night in camp, as the party feasted on the "best and sweetest meat" of the ewe, Apikuni declared, "That mountain shall be called Singleshot Mountain from this day forth"—one of the few names that he actually gave to the area.

Two days later Grinnell, Apikuni and Yellowfish moved along upper St. Mary Lake and set up camp in a driving rainstorm. Hunting became a necessity for them when they discovered Yellowfish had forgotten to pack the leftover sheep meat, leaving them only some damp bread and a few half-dried fish for subsistence. They followed a game trail up the creek at the southwestern end of Singleshot Mountain and named the stream Rose Creek for Yellowfish. His Blackfoot name, *Otokomi*, was given to the mountain where he now hunted. Leading their horses up a game trail worn into a precipitous ledge they dubbed Golden Stairs, Grinnell and Apikuni looked for game on the "Goat Mountain" to the south. Working their way carefully over the ledges, "skirting the deep but narrow cañon whose vertical walls dropped off sheer for nearly 1,000 feet," they saw neither game nor sign. Yellowfish, a distant speck toward Singleshot Mountain, was the only moving object they could find. Discouraged and hungry, they climbed down and returned to camp.

From the bench on Goat Mountain, Grinnell identified the "narrows" in the upper lake and saw the dim shadows of half a dozen stupendous mountains through a veil of driving rain. On the southern end of Goat Mountain he observed "a great mass of bluish white which looks like a tremendous glacier."

The discomfort of wet clothes and an unsavory meal of scorched fish and soggy bread persuaded Apikuni and Yellowfish that they should return to their camp on the inlet to Lower St. Mary Lake. Grinnell reluctantly agreed. Traveling rapidly, they reached their camp at 9 P.M., cold, wet and hungry, after riding forty miles and walking ten that day.

The next day Grinnell and Apikuni fished the lower lake; Grinnell caught a five-and-a-half pound lake trout, then a "small one" of four pounds with his fly rod. Trolling, Apikuni caught three more, one of which weighed nine pounds, then boasted he had netted one weighing thirty-five pounds the year before. Further, he claimed a trapper had landed one "so large that when its captor ran a stick through its gills to carry it over his shoulder, its tail dragged on the ground as he walked to camp."

Hunting Glaciers

On September 14 the group left camp for a two-day exploration of the Swiftcurrent, a name coined by Grinnell after learning the Blackfeet term for it meant swift-flowing river; ". . . its fall is very rapid, and there are no quiet pools . . . near where it pours into the St. Mary's. The water is cold as ice." Grinnell noted immediately the difference between this water and usual clear mountain streams: the pale, greenish tint hinted to the stream's glacial origins. As they advanced up the valley, the mountain slopes changed to vertical walls 3,000-4,000 feet high, fringed at their bases with fine talus. At intervals, narrow canyons led to wide cirques created by ancient glaciers. Farther up the valley, "a superb glacier came into view."[9]

They camped in a patch of green timber just below the falls at the outlet of the fifth lake, later to be named Swiftcurrent. The falls disappointed Grinnell, who described them only as a "series of broken cascades, each about twenty-five feet high." From a high point they surveyed the hourglass-shaped lake; beyond it, they found a sixth lake (Josephine), its waters "very green and milky." Between the lakes stood a great mountain with a triangular base, "two of its sides facing the lakes being cut away vertically." Various rock strata, black, dull green, dark red and purple, formed prominent ledges on the mountain's sides. Above the sixth lake, they could see the glacier "at least a mile in width," its ice, several hundred feet thick and extending back to the summit of the mountain, broken in two as it flowed over a tremendous cliff.[10]

Grinnell rose before dawn, anxious to start for the glacier. Apikuni accompanied him, while Yellowfish went hunting. At the edge of the fifth lake they considered possible routes and finally decided to stay on its east side. Just as they set out, Apikuni spotted two goats halfway up a great mountain (Allen) to their south and excitedly argued that they should pursue the game. Although Grinnell came to hunt, he would not be deterred: reaching the ice "just then seemed to me much more important than to kill a goat."

They followed game trails beyond the fifth lake, hoping to find a good place to ford the stream. Off the game trail they could not penetrate the thick, entangled timber, so they tried several other trails, all of which eventually turned away from their objective. Finally they broke through the brush and timber and worked their way up a steep, slippery slope to the first ledge on the flank of the great triangular mountain.

Angry clouds rushed toward them, hiding the mountains in a sheet of driving rain that intermittently changed to snow. They began to climb hand over hand, up the ledges rising one above the other in a seemingly endless series, following each narrow bench until they found a place where they could scale the next ledge. All the while the wind blew furiously, threatening to blow the climbers off the narrow ledges. One side offered only smooth rock to cling to; the other dropped vertically from twenty to two hundred feet. Grinnell wrote:

> At one place where a gust rushing down a narrow gorge caught me I positively flattened myself against the rock. Appekunny had seated himself after a bit of rough scrambling, and I had gone on along a ledge to see what it led to. The ledge was only ten or twelve inches wide, and beneath was a drop of perhaps forty feet, while my shoulder brushed against the cliff that towered I knew not how far above me. A sheep trail followed the ledge and led me to hope the way would be an easy one to ascend. After going thirty or forty yards, I came to a narrow gorge only six or eight feet wide, and the trail turned sharply at right angles about a projecting point of rock, the path being so narrow that I had to exercise a good deal of care to turn the corner without falling off.
>
> As I rounded it the wind caught me with a violence that for a moment sent my heart into my mouth. Back from the corner ran

a deep narrow chasm or cañon, cut out by a small mountain stream, and twenty feet in front of me the ledge on which I was walking ran out, and the sheep trail crossed the chasm. The distance across was only four or five feet—an easy leap for a sheep or for an ordinarily active man—but the landing place on the other side was on another narrow ledge about eight or ten inches wide and broken down on its outer side for several inches into a sharp slope to the edge of the cliff. Forty or fifty feet below I could see the gleam of the stream, and in the lulls of the wind hear the tinkle of the waters as they fell from rock to rock.

The jump might well enough be made in the excitement of pursuit or flight, but I did not feel like attempting it in cold blood. One would have to alight on his feet just rightly balanced. If he went too far he would strike the cliff with his body and might rebound and fall off; if he did not go quite far enough, of course he would lose his balance and fall. I looked at the jump for a moment or two and then very gingerly turning myself about, went back to look for an easier way.

By the time the pair had climbed nearly to the top of the mountain, they found themselves on the edge of a huge amphitheater of rock. Down through the middle of this immense rock basin "foamed a great torrent, the sum of a thousand springs which trickled from the rocks, and as many rivulets, which crept out from beneath the snow banks. . . ." Grinnell could now see additional lakes in the Swiftcurrent chain, at least eleven in a continuous series. He also had an excellent view of the northern part of the glacier, its vertical face fluted as it fell over a great cliff.

Realizing they could not reach the glacier from this approach, they climbed slowly down the mountain to camp—tired, wet and hungry, once again without game. Yellowfish had been there since noon after firing all his ammunition, about twenty rounds, without hitting a single goat. He felt he was bewitched: "Some moons it is so—a man cannot shoot—and when it happens so, one knows that the medicine is bad."

They had no food; breakfast on the morning of September 16, 1885, consisted of "whittling up a pipeful of tobacco apiece." Shouldering their rifles, they headed to the steep mountain (Altyn Peak) north of camp where Yellowfish had hunted the day before. From the foot of the talus slope beneath the vertical cliffs, they spotted a ewe and her kid on a ledge far above them. Grinnell clambered up the slope about a hundred yards as fast as he could. Out of breath and unable to steady his rifle, he fired and missed. The goats disappeared behind some rocks, then climbed an almost vertical ravine eight hundred yards above.[11]

A half mile farther, they entered a canyon that led to a small basin divided by a stream cascading over a series of falls. They named the stream for Apikuni, who decided to return to camp because his rubber boots would be too dangerous on the vertical walls and narrow ledges that lay ahead. Yellowfish and Grinnell continued on, one man climbing up six or eight feet to the next narrow ledge while the other held both rifles and then passed them up. Conquering the first wall, they passed along a steep, half-frozen slope of shale to the next rock face where a crevice allowed them to brace their backs and feet against the sides. The top gained, they moved to the next and repeated the process several times.

Grinnell became extremely tired during the difficult climb and his legs "seemed almost incapable of motion." At a bench with a small alpine lake, Yellowfish suggested the best way back to camp was over a high saddle to the south, just west of the mountain's summit. Grinnell, in spite of his fatigue, was determined to follow so long as he could "put one foot before the other." On a higher bench they passed another lake—its surface frozen and swept clear by the bitter wind that blew across the basin—and named it *Natahki* (Fine Shield Woman) for Apikuni's Piegan wife. Slowly they climbed across a snow field that led to the saddle (between Altyn Peak and Mount Henkel). Adding to Grinnell's misery, his shoes had been torn apart by the rock climbing; as he broke through the crusted snow, the ice cut his feet.

At last they stood on the top of the ridge and looked at the Swiftcurrent valley below, all the lakes above the fourth one visible in the bright sunshine, the stream shining "like a band of polished metal." A great flock of gray-crowned finches feeding along the ridge, "cheery and comfortable looking as they always are, . . . fluttered and hopped about us in the most confiding way." They descended a steep, snow-covered slope of sliding shale interrupted by vertical ledges that made the travel slow and difficult. They flushed two blue grouse and Yellowfish shot one, then carried it back to camp where "long before it was cold, [the bird] was roasting over the hot fire, and soon devoured." With nothing more to eat, the three men packed up and left for the St. Mary lakes. As they crossed the last ridge before going down the valley, Grinnell looked back and could see only black clouds and whirling snow.

Above Grinnell Glacier, 1926.

Over the next two days Grinnell lounged in camp, visited the nearby Kootenai camp, and rode down the St. Mary River valley to get a closer view of the "grand needle of rock," Chief Mountain. He caught several trout and, on cleaning them, found they were feeding on meadow mice. The discovery "greatly disgusted Appekunny, who foreswore trout from that time, and spoke of them thereafter in most indignant and contemptuous terms."

After considerable discussion, the hunters—except for the superstitious Yellowfish—agreed that the earliness of the season was to blame for their poor hunting; the game remained high on their summer range, not yet driven by winter weather toward the lakes. Yellowfish struck out for the agency a day ahead of Grinnell and Apikuni, certain he had been visited by "bad medicine."

Late in the first afternoon of the three-day journey back to the agency, Grinnell and Apikuni crossed the St. Mary Ridge and camped atop a bluff on the South Fork of the Milk River. A fierce wind challenged their abilities to set up the tent and fix dinner. During the night the wind prevailed, blowing down their tent; they did not bother to raise it again, but slept under it until dawn. On the last day of their trip, just north of Two Medicine Lodge Creek, they met a group of Piegan riders led by Many Tail Feathers. "Many horses stolen," he explained; raiding Crows had taken 150-200 head during the night. Once the trail was found, a party of about twenty-five galloped after the thieves, even though they had a twelve-hour head start. The Blackfeet returned the next day on exhausted mounts, driving the regained horses before them.

Bear Pipe Dance

Grinnell remembered his promise to Yellowfish to give a Bear Pipe dance when he returned to the agency if his hunt had been successful. Accordingly, Grinnell, Apikuni and Joseph Kipp, the owner of the trading post at the agency, rode over to Red Eagle's camp on the Two Medicine. Red Eagle, Fine Shield Woman's uncle, owned the Bear Pipe and was "the most potent of the medicine men of the Pegunny." The white men brought gifts of tea, bread, tobacco and dried serviceberries, then waited while last-minute preparations for the ceremony were made. Finally, Red Eagle called them into the lodge.

Red Eagle, a "large, fine looking man of majestic presence" and blind from extreme age, sat at the back with the fire between him and the door. The white men sat to his left, in the place of honor. Bear Woman, the medicine man's wife, placed a fiery coal in front of him as he began a low, plaintive, monotonous chant. Bear Woman occasionally dropped dried, sweet-smelling pine needles on the coal, filling the lodge with fragrance.

Both Bear Woman and Red Eagle grasped handfuls of smoke and rubbed them over his head, shoulders and arms, then swallowed some. Raising his blind eyes, Red Eagle prayed for health and long life of the assembled group: ". . . Let the young people grow; increase their flesh. Let all men, women and children have full life. Harden the bodies of the old people so that they may reach great age." Smoke was then applied to a large bundle tied to a decorated pack saddle that hung overhead from the lodge poles.

Red Eagle began a new song, more lively than before, and moved his hands through the smoke to represent the antelope, the bear and the buffalo. When the song ended, he removed the bundle's outer red cloth wrapping slowly, carefully, then he peeled away ten or twelve silk handkerchiefs of various colors to reveal the Bear Pipe. Grinnell noted that it had

> a handsome stem about four feet long, wrapped for a part of its length with large handsome beads, and profusely ornamented with white weasel tails and feathers, which depended from it in thick bunches. Near the lower or pipe extremity was a spread plume of twelve tail feathers of the war eagle, each one having its extremity wrapped with red or yellow horse hair, which hung down in a long tuft. Below this plume the stem was tied with red, green and yellow ribbons, and again below this was a cluster of brightly burnished hawks bells. The whole stem was very handsome and heavy.

After pressing his lips to the pipe and offering another prayer, Red Eagle passed it to Apikuni, who handed it on to Grinnell. Around the circle it went, each man earnestly praying to it. When it returned to Red Eagle, he said rapidly, twenty or thirty times, "pity, pity," and danced to the east, then to the west. Sitting down, he repeated his original prayers and concluded, "Let the Sun shine upon us and our lives be without shadows." The people countered, "Yes, have pity, have pity." The Bear Pipe dance was over.

Back at the agency, Grinnell spoke to the agent, Major R. A. Allen, about his management of Indian affairs. Allen and Almost-a-Dog, an old chief, told him about the Starvation Winter of 1883-84; Almost-a-Dog cut notches on a stick to tally the dead that winter. Grinnell noted in his diary that the Indians "are willing to work, but sadly need instruction." He thought farmers and mechanics should be hired, about one to every twenty-five Indian families, to teach them how to work to their best advantage.[12]

Two days later, as Grinnell sat in Kipp's store, he heard Four Bears, the camp orator, brag of his powerful medicine. With expressive gestures, the garrulous old Indian explained how he could part his ribs and have a wagon roll out onto the prairie. Also, he could not be hurt in war: ". . . if the bullets hit me they will not go through my skin, they will glance off. I cannot be hurt by them."

They moved outdoors behind the store so he could show some of his magic to Grinnell. After tooting a whistle made from the leg bone of a beaver, Four Bears took a mouthful of water and blew it in a fine spray into the air, then seemed to vomit into his hand. The first two times he did this, his hand appeared wet but empty; the third time, he held a polished pebble of white quartz. Grinnell thought the exhibition worth a present and went back into the store to purchase a plug of tobacco.

Eager to receive a gift from such an important white man, the pompous Four Bears declared he would give Grinnell a name. He took him by the hand and led him out into the sunlight, then threw Grinnell's cap on the ground and began to pray:

> Oh Sun, oh Old Man, look down. Have pity . . . . when I was a young man, I went upon the top of the Sweet Grass Buttes, where all the Indians are afraid to go . . . while I slept my medicine said to me, "Take the name Pe-nut-u-ye is-tsim-o-kam [Fisher Cap]." . . . I do not longer need this name, and now I give it to this my son. Pity him. Give him long life. . . . Hear, Sun; hear Old Man; pity, pity.

During the prayer, Four Bears grabbed at the sunlight and rubbed it over Grinnell's head, shoulders, arms and chest. "That is what you are called—Pe-nut-u-ye is-tsim-o-kam." The ceremony over, Grinnell gave Four Bears his well-earned tobacco.

During his last day with the Blackfeet, Grinnell watched them harvest grain; they operated the huge threshing machine with considerable incompetence, confirming his belief that the Indians needed instruction. Later he rode with Schultz and Kipp to the high bluffs along the south side of Badger Creek, an area used by the Blackfeet as a burial ground, and examined Bull Chief's grave. He wrote in his diary, "There were a lot of quilts and coats on the coffin and I wanted to get into them but S & K were uneasy and thought there was a fresh body in there so I did not disturb them."

As Grinnell prepared to leave for home, he mused:

> The last nights in camp are to me rather sad, full of memories in which the bitter and sweet are oddly commingled. . . . The recollection of these days and their joys is full of pleasure. . . . The

return to civilization is like the return to his dungeon of a prisoner who has been shown a glimpse of freedom. . . . The old rifle has had its final cleaning and is put away, the knife is rusting in its sheath. . . . Yo.

Clearly, from Grinnell's description, he came to hunt and live the outdoor life, not to check on the condition of the Blackfeet after the Starvation Winter of 1883-84, as later suggested by Schultz. Apikuni may fairly be credited with first drawing Grinnell's attention to the St. Mary Lake region by his description of it in *Forest and Stream*. Afterwards, though, his presence becomes less significant to Grinnell, and Schultz ultimately became a vexation to him.

The 1885 trip reawakened Grinnell's interest in Indians, a curiosity that had diminished in the thirteen years since his summer with the Pawnee. With renewed dedication, he began to collect Pawnee folk tales and devoted parts of his summers to studying the Blackfeet and Cheyenne.

Finally, as an out-of-doors enthusiast, Grinnell was stirred by the beauty and ruggedness of the St. Mary region:

An artist's palette, splashed with all the hues of his color box, would not have shown more varied contrasts. The rocks were of all shades, from pale gray, through green and pink, to dark red, purple and black, and against them stood out the pale foliage of the willows, the bright gold of the aspens and cottonwoods, the vivid red of the mountain maples and ash, and the black of the pines. In the valley were the greens of the deciduous shrubs, great patches of the deep maroon of the changing lobelia, lakes, turbid or darkly blue, sombre evergreens; on the mountain side foaming cascades, with their white whirling mist wreathes, gray blue ice masses, and fields of gleaming snow. Over all arched a leaden sky, whose shadows might dull, but could never efface, the bewildering beauty of this mass of color.

He would taste the grandeur over and over in the years to come.

"Looked down into a seemingly bottomless abyss."

IV

"The Rock Climbers," 1887

O N FEBRUARY 11, 1886, *Forest and Stream* announced the founding of the Audubon Society, an organization dedicated to "saving the birds of this continent, and especially song and other small birds. . . ."

In an article a month earlier, Grinnell blamed the rapid disappearance of birds from orchards, woods and fields on a fashion fad, stating "nearly all the ladies wore bird skins or heads or wings; many men went shooting small birds to make money by selling the skins, and innumerable boys went bird nesting." By the end of the year, the new organization had over twenty thousand members in North America, Europe and Asia.

Grinnell did not return to the St. Mary region in 1886. He wrote to James Willard Schultz in August, wishing Apikuni good luck hunting bears: "Don't kill 'em all; save a few for me next year." In September Grinnell hunted elk in Yellowstone (legal until 1894) before moving on to his Shirley Basin ranch, where he met his old friend Luther North and George H. Gould, a California banker. Gould's brother, Charles, a New York attorney, had been a classmate of Grinnell's at Yale. In November Grinnell wrote Schultz that hunting that fall was "all business . . . an elk or two, a few deer and a few antelope being all that I killed."

The following year he longed for another trip to the land of glaciers. "You don't want an extra packer or guide for your trip do you?" Grinnell asked Joseph Kipp in a January letter. "I am open to any offers for any position except cook." A month later he wrote to North and Gould, pleading for their company on an outing to the Chief

Mountain country in October: "We must make that trip, old fellow, for you and I are getting so old [Grinnell was thirty-seven!] that we cannot make many more trips. This one, I think, would be a grand one to finish off with, and I want to make it, and in your company." At the last minute North declined, but Gould agreed to go.

The Canadian Pacific had completed its transcontinental line two years earlier, so Grinnell could now travel from Montreal to Lethbridge, Alberta, about sixty-five miles north of the St. Mary country, in considerable comfort. Adding to this convenience, he secured a pass from the railroad to travel free as a journalist. Similar arrangements were made from Vancouver for his "San Francisco correspondent," Gould. As he had in 1885, Grinnell planned to write about his experiences in the Montana mountains for *Forest and Stream*; this time he grouped his several episodes under the general title of "The Rock Climbers."

The first published map of the St. Mary region, compiled by Grinnell in 1885 and 1887. —Forest and Stream, May 24, 1888

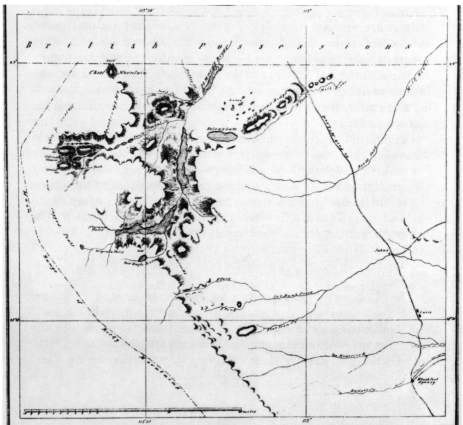

Schultz agreed to meet Grinnell and Gould with a wagon at Lethbridge for the five- or six-day trip to the lakes. Primed for what lay ahead, Grinnell wrote for the first installment of his series how he would "behold once more the beauties of these mountains, to live over again . . . the old free life of other days . . . and thus to regain lost vigor." Although he had confessed to Schultz the previous fall that he would like to kill a couple of goats just to say he had done so, he revealed his main motive for this trip in a June letter to John George "Kootenay" Brown: ". . . to spend a month or two among those stupendous mountains and to see something of the ice rivers which rise on their summits."

As scheduled, the three men met in Lethbridge on October 1; by October 8 they had reached Lower St. Mary Lake and found a boat that Schultz had cached there the year before. They agreed they would need another man to help with hunting, so Grinnell volunteered to ride to a "whiskey trader's camp" on Pike Lake near the Canadian border while his companions moved their camp down to the lake's inlet.

J. B. "Jack" Monroe was away when Grinnell arrived at his camp late in the afternoon but returned soon after dark. In the meantime, Grinnell learned something about the brisk trade in whiskey across the border, marked only by piles of stones on the ridge a quarter mile away. Liquor was illegal in the western Canadian territories, and in great demand; a gallon that sold for $2 in the United States brought $20 in Alberta. But the risks were also high—the Northwest Mounted Police patrolled constantly and the penalties were severe.

Back at Grinnell's camp on the west side of the upper lake, the men paired up for hunting—Grinnell with Schultz and Gould with Monroe. Some of the unhonored mountains of 1885 now received names: Otokomi, Goat, Going-to-the-Sun and, across the lake, Kootenai and Divide.[13] They found no game after several days on (East) Flattop, Singleshot and Red Eagle, then spotted "moving specks" of goats on Goat Mountain. The next day in Rose Basin, when the camp needed meat, Grinnell got his first "fair shot" at a goat on a little shelf. After taking a "careful and rather long aim," Grinnell wrote,

> . . . the shot rang out. . . . The goat sprang to its feet . . . [and] ran to the edge of the shelf as if about to leap off. . . . It turned and ran back to the crevice . . . and reared against the rocks as if to try to ascend, . . . and it ran back to the edge of the shelf. . . . Its knees gave way and it pitched forward, whirling over and over through the air, struck a ledge and bounded out again, . . . down the mountainside and out of sight.

"Hurrah!" shouted Appekunny, "You've got him, sure enough, and you ought to, for you took long enough to aim."

By the time they butchered the goat and divided the load between them, it was dusk and raining. As the evening grew dim, they hung their prize in a tree and picked their way back to the horses through deep ravines filled with brush and slide rock. The pitch black night made it impossible to follow the trail back to camp, so they stayed on the mountainside without food or water. All night they heard noisy geese on the lake not far below.

Gould and Monroe hunted on the north side of the upper lake. Gould fired several times at what he believed to be a black bear; his aim was true but the "bear" turned out to be a black stump. Meanwhile, Grinnell and Schultz followed a well-defined Kootenai hunting trail on a side trip to Red Eagle Lake, where, on the steep, step-like

This photo from the Morton J. Elrod Collection shows the trail that leads to Grinnell Glacier, ca. 1926.

ledges south of the lake, Grinnell shot two goats but recovered only one. As he and Schultz carried it out, a violent blizzard forced their return to the camp at St. Mary Lake; they barely survived, leading their horses through knee-deep snow into a wind the animals refused to face. "Darkness was closing over the lake when they reached the camp, but half an hour later, when warm and with dry clothing they were enjoying their delicious supper, they laughed at the hardships of the day's march."

Bitter cold followed the blizzard for three days and the men kept near the fire until a chinook arrived. Gould, still unsuccessful in the hunt, claimed he had to return home for scheduled business appointments; Grinnell thought there might be another reason, recounting what Gould had told him earlier:

> I am a follower of St. Paul, being obliged for my health's sake to take each day a certain fixed quantity of spirit. . . . At Lethbridge I had for sanitary purposes bought two gallons of whiskey at a great price. . . . Some bottles were smashed in transit; we stopped over night in a snow storm at the house of a philosopher, who . . . drank three bottles, . . . and some of the liquor, too, was used up in a way . . . I can almost call legitimate, but all was gone.

Gould and Jack Monroe left for Lethbridge on October 26; Grinnell and Schultz continued hunting for sheep on Flattop and Singleshot without luck. One morning Grinnell spotted with binoculars a mounted rider leading a four-horse team hitched to a sky-blue wagon , followed by several men on foot—"a soldier outfit." Lt. John H. Beacom and the Third Infantry from Fort Shaw visited the hunters' camp the next day. After an enjoyable chat and receiving "all the latest news from the States," Grinnell, Schultz and Beacom rode up the lake to take some photographs with Grinnell's camera. Finding Beacom congenial, Schultz and Grinnell invited him to join them on a trip up the Swiftcurrent. After Monroe's return from Lethbridge, the party ferried their supplies to the foot of the lower lake, cached all but a week's provisions, which they loaded on two mules, and headed up the Swiftcurrent. It was quite dark by the time they found a good camp two miles below the fifth lake.

The next morning the camp rose before dawn.

> There was no sound heard but the crackling of the fire. . . . Presently Jack marched up to the fire with an armful of wood. As he threw it down he said:
> "Yo [Grinnell] reminds me of Gwenwynwyn the Bold."
> "How so?" grunted Appekunny, who was kneading the bread for breakfast in the spare frying pan.

"Why, don't you know?" said Jack, "the Welsh hero 'sought night and day the philosopher's stone,' and Yo is just as bad about glaciers. He has been talking about them more or less ever since we've been out, and durned if I don't believe he dreams about 'em nights."

The four men rode past the frowning face of Apikuni Mountain and the old campground beneath the falls at the outlet of the fifth lake. Looking for a pathway to the glacier, they plunged into the forest along its north shore through thickets of willows, soft boggy mires and down timber. An old Indian trail led up a narrow valley toward the ice, then along a natural avenue between the tapered spruces to the vertical face of the huge mountain that stood between the two branches of the Swiftcurrent. They soon emerged on a bare hillside, leading their horses along a little-used game trail to the head of the sixth lake, called Grinnell then, but now Josephine. The glacier lay just ahead; below it, the mountain fell away in a sheer precipice.

After Grinnell took several photographs of the glacier from the head of the lake, they began picking their way through the drift timber blocking the stream bed. Half a mile up they came to the edge of a huge avalanche that blocked their way with broken and splintered logs. A marvelous view of the ice prompted more photographs. Since it was getting late, they returned to their camp to make another attempt the next day. At the head of the lake the party divided—Beacom and Grinnell returned over their previous route while Schultz and Monroe followed the southern shore and found a good trail that took them quickly and easily to camp.

With two mules and five days' worth of supplies, the party made a fresh start the next day for the glacier above the lake. The lake already bore Grinnell's name, and now Beacom suggested naming the glacier after him as well, but Grinnell protested. Unable to climb because of an old injury, Beacom returned to his camp at Lower St. Mary Lake; the other three men continued up the trail on a path so narrow it tore the packs on the mules to pieces and left "fragments of bedding dangling from the branches and tree trunks."

They left on foot before daylight the next morning, moving along the east side of the stream above Grinnell Lake. Schultz carried the camera on his back, Monroe toted the shotgun and Grinnell packed a cartridge belt and rifle. Before long they reached a wide, rapid mountain stream that entered from the southwest; Grinnell named it Cataract Creek.

Soon they stood on the shore of a beautiful, circular glacial lake just below the glacier, "while on the north and the south were stern snow-wreathed rock walls which seemed to forbid further progress. . . . A

Grinnell Glacier, 1887, as seen from the creek between Lake Josephine and Grinnell Lake by Grinnell and Lt. Beacom, probably taken by Grinnell but credited to Beacom. —Glacier National Park

low, rocky pine-crowned promontory" jutted from the south side. On the west, the path to the ice was blocked by "a thousand feet of black precipice, divided into two nearly equal halves by the white waving line of foam" formed by the stream that flowed from beneath the glacier. To the north, a lofty mountain rose "abruptly in a series of rocky ledges," ending in "a knife edge of naked pinnacled rock, cold, hard and forbidding." After shooting more photographs they moved cautiously over the rocky talus of the eastern promontory and reached a swampy meadow at the base of the falls. Tangled willow, great bars of gray gravel and debris from the glacier above checked their progress. Determined, they attacked the cliff, using old channels of the waterfall to find crevices and projections for foot and handholds until they finally reached the lower edge of the glacier.[14]

The glacier lay in a basin two miles wide and three miles long. The lower edge of the glacier had no snow for a half mile; its grayish-blue ice gleamed in the bright sunshine. The smaller, uppermost portion of the glacier spilled over a rock ledge before joining the massive lower section. Snow covered the top, dotted here and there with stones and dirt. At the sides, huge blocks of fractured ice "shone like sapphires."

In his diary Grinnell estimated the thickness of the lower mass at seven hundred feet, the upper at three hundred. He also noted the glacier's laminated character, produced by annual layers of compacted surface dirt between each winter's snow. The whole glacier occupied about three thousand vertical feet on the mountainside.

The men spent several hours climbing on the glacier. Close to the cliff where the glacier's upper portion joined its lower mass, they looked down into "a seemingly bottomless abyss, where the ice had melted next to the rock." Soft, fresh snow near the edge offered good footing, but they could not negotiate the glare ice near the middle of the glacier. Schultz carelessly tried to take a shortcut across an area of hardened snow; he slipped and tobogganed down the steep slope, stopping on some soft snow "after going about a hundred yards at a high rate of speed."

They ate bread and cheese for lunch at the foot of a great moraine, then returned to the ice by a game trail that led up to the surface,

Mount Gould as it appeared, ca. 1926.

where they discovered fresh sheep tracks. As they rounded a rocky point, Schultz exclaimed, "Jesus Christ, look at that ram!"

A bighorn stood on the snow, outlined against the sky. "How far, Jack?" Grinnell asked.

"About two hundred [yards]," Monroe replied.

Grinnell dropped to one knee and fired. They lost sight of the animal and hurried up the slope, Monroe in the lead. "Hurrah, Mr. G., blood on the snow and lots of it."

Excited, Grinnell tried to follow the bloody trail and scrambled up a rocky ledge, then forced his way through a waist-deep snow drift. The work exhausted his adrenaline rush. Breathless, he turned the task of tracking over to Monroe and returned with Schultz to explore the glacier, again more interested in this marvel of nature than in hunting. Monroe worked his way down the rough precipices and, after about a mile, found the ram lying down. When he approached, the sheep rose, staggered a few steps and fell dead over a ledge into a snowbank. Grinnell wrote:

> He was a beauty. Four years old with a coat that was perfection brown and smooth, a pair of horns not very large, but perfectly symmetrical, short of limb, strong of back, sturdy and stout, plump and round. . . . He was very fat and just the meat we needed.

Under an overcast sky, the wind began to howl across the peaks, warning the men of an impending snowstorm. Grinnell and Schultz took a few more photographs, then started down the mountain, following the smoke of a fire in the little valley below where Monroe was roasting some of the sheep's fat ribs—"the best piece of meat in the mountains."

With their photographic equipment, they could carry only the ram's shoulders back to camp that day. On the mountain to the north, later called Mount Grinnell, they found an easier route down than the one they used for their ascent, so they followed it back to camp. Schultz and Monroe returned the next day to collect the remainder of the sheep. The weather continued to deteriorate, so they returned to their camp at the foot of Lower St. Mary Lake just in time to bid Lieutenant Beacom goodbye. Grinnell gave the young officer a sketch-map of the area, and Beacom replenished the camp's supply of sugar, bacon and coffee.

Bad weather persisted and prevented more hunting. Snow fell daily and the wind blew bitter cold with a rare ferocity—the tops of fifty-foot pines and spruces bent horizontal and birds were thrown to the ground when they tried to fly. The men sat in their tent, day after day, in awe of the noise. Grinnell wrote in his diary:

Last night the wind blew a perfect tornado, and I thought that the tent would go down at any minute. The rattling of the stovepipe against the poles, the noise of Appekunny's swinging yeast can, the pounding of the waves on the beach, the rush of the wind through the trees and the flapping of the canvas made a noise which made it hopeless to try to sleep.

After ten days of stormy weather and over a half foot of snow, the hunters surrendered and headed for Lethbridge.

Out in the open . . . the fury of the wind was felt in its full force. . . . Sometimes it took me up out of the saddle and threw me forward on the horse's neck. . . . My horse was often thrown to one side by a gust. . . . Dung from Jack's horse, voided as he walked along, was caught as it fell and whirled away as if it were bits of pepper. Down in the stream, I saw water caught up by the barrelsful and whirled away into the air first as white spray, then as mist, then as nothing.

The Garden Wall towers above Grinnell Glacier in this photo from the Morton J. Elrod Collection, ca. 1926.

They spent the first night at Sam Bird's ranch house on the South Fork of the Milk River. The sixteen-foot square cabin sheltered the three hunters, three ranch hands, a woman and her baby, uncounted cats, dogs and hens, and one rooster. "The rooster crowed pretty much all night and the baby cried." Intimidated by this civilized setting, Jack Monroe left for his camp the next morning. Grinnell and Schultz continued on, crossing into Canada later in the mid-November day.

At the station at the crossing of St. Mary River, the Northwest Mounted Police passed Schultz and Grinnell through without incident, and the two plodded on, slowed only by the wagon's pace. The next afternoon, the same Mounties overtook them after receiving a tip that Grinnell was smuggling whiskey. When the search produced no evidence, the police suspected the informant, a whiskey trader himself, had probably transported his own contraband across the boundary during the diversion.

During a visit to Victoria, British Columbia, before heading home, Grinnell received public praise and was credited with discovering the first glacier in the United States, though Clarence King had claimed that honor over a decade earlier. Meanwhile, in a letter to Gould, Grinnell added more names to the geographic features in the area.

> Gould's Mountain and Grinnell's Basin will probably appear on a map of the St. Mary's region, which is to be made by a young army officer who was with us for a day or two about the Lakes. He went up Swift Current with us and from afar saw the glories of my glacier, and after my return I saw him again and made a diagram of the country. . . . The reason I possess a basin and a glacier is because this young man insisted in naming both after me. I, having secured these pieces of property, could do no less than sprinkle the names of other members of [the] party over the adjacent territory.

Always humble, and probably a bit embarrassed about having his name on maps of areas he had explored, Grinnell must have felt some atonement when, in 1917, he received an excerpt from Lieutenant Beacom's diary of October-November 1887, which read:

> I had the good fortune to fall in with Mr. Grinnell, Natural History Editor of *Forest and Stream*, and I enjoyed his hospitality and society for three days. I accompanied him up Swift Current and we photographed the glacier at the head of that stream, which in honor of him I called Grinnell Glacier.[15]

In the next few years, Grinnell refined his map and named more landmarks in the St. Mary country.

Grinnell and Luther North take a bighorn sheep on Singleshot Mountain.

V

"Slide Rock from Many Mountains," 1891

O N AN EVENING IN DECEMBER 1887, eleven men gathered around the dining table at Theodore Roosevelt's Madison Avenue home to discuss the formation of a sportsman's association. Like Roosevelt, George Bird Grinnell and the other men present were avid hunters, came from venerable New England families, had been educated at Ivy League schools, were wealthy or financially well-off, and were influential New York leaders.

The other men in attendance included Roosevelt's brother Elliott and cousin J. West Roosevelt, Archibald Rogers and E. P. Rogers, J. Coleman Drayton, Thomas Paton, James E. Jones, John J. Pierrepont and Rutherford Stuyvesant. They appointed Grinnell, Roosevelt and Archibald Rogers to formulate the organization's goals, which emit the distinct spirit of Grinnell:

(1) To promote manly sport with the rifle.

(2) To promote travel and exploration in the wild and unknown, or but partially known, portions of the country.

(3) To work for the preservation of the large game of this country, and, so far as possible, to further legislation for that purpose, and to assist in enforcing the existing laws.

(4) To promote inquiry into, and to record observations on the habits and natural history of, the various wild animals.

(5) To bring about among the members the interchange of opinions and ideas on hunting, travel, and exploration; on the various kinds of hunting rifles; on the haunts of game animals, etc.

This meeting marked the beginning of the Boone and Crockett Club, named for America's most famous hunters and the first of its kind in the United States.

As early as May 1884 Grinnell had advocated in *Forest and Stream* an "association of men bound together by their interest in game and fish, to take active charge of all matters pertaining to the enactment and carrying out of laws on the subject." In subsequent editorials he campaigned against killing game animals in traps and using torches to hunt at night, emphasizing "fair chase" and the "code of the sportsman."

Grinnell also promoted these ideas in 1885, when Roosevelt called upon him at *Forest and Stream* to discuss the review he had written of the future president's book, *Hunting Trips of a Ranchman.* Grinnell had complimented the author for his "exceptionally well-balanced mind, and calm deliberate judgement," but he suggested that Roosevelt's limited experience in the West lent only charm and freshness to the book. However, he said, "We are sorry to see that a number of hunting myths are given as fact. . . ." That Grinnell appeased Roosevelt at all is a tribute to his social skills. He recalled their meeting in his "Introduction" to the twenty-volume *Works of Theodore Roosevelt*:

> . . . we talked freely about the book, and took up at length some of its statements. He at once saw my point of view, and after we had discussed the book . . . passed on to the broader subject of hunting in the West. . . . My account of big-game destruction much impressed Roosevelt, and gave him his first direct and detailed information about this slaughter of elk, deer, antelope, and mountain-sheep. No doubt it had some influence in making him the ardent game protector that he later became, just as my own experiences had started me along the same road.

For his contributions to the Boone and Crockett Club Grinnell deserves more than the title of charter member or co-founder. All of the members agreed he was the most active and influential. He formulated almost every idea the club came to stand for; he introduced to the group most of the issues it became involved in; he did most of the work on the Boone and Crockett hunting and conservation book series; and he effectively used *Forest and Stream* to speak for the club in its long campaign to protect Yellowstone National Park. And Grinnell alone furthered the association's aim to explore the only "wild and unknown . . . portions of the country" that still existed, the St. Mary region.

Getting to Know the Unknown

Grinnell returned to the St. Mary country in the fall of 1888. This time, in addition to his usual camp gear and rifle, he carried a barometer. At every opportunity he measured altitudes and took bearings on mountaintops to improve the map he had started the year before. George Gould accompanied him again, along with James Willard Schultz and Jack Monroe, and this time he had persuaded his old friend Luther North to join them.

They headed first up the Swiftcurrent. Grinnell logged in his diary: "Lute killed a goat which fell 1000 feet and was lost behind a waterfall." Gould, finally triumphant, killed one as well. Grinnell again was less interested in hunting than in glaciers. He quickly realized that the glacier Lieutenant Beacom had named in his honor the year before was melting rapidly and had diminished in size. He wrote:

> The glacier was vocal with the sound of running water. The musical tinkle of the tiny rivulet, the deep bass roar of the dashing torrent, the hiss of rushing water, confined as in a flume, fell upon the ear, and up through the holes and crevasses in the ice came strange hollow murmurs, growlings and roarings. . . . [Grinnell,] very anxious to reach the crest of the mountain . . . started up the slope, walking carefully. . . . The ice grew more and more steep and more and more slippery. . . . It was each moment more difficult to [walk across]. . . . A wide chasm yawned between the ice and *terra firma*—a chasm too wide to be jumped. . . . A slip of the foot might result in a fall, and the man if he fell would go sliding down the ice with no hope of stopping before the crevasses were reached. . . . [Grinnell continued] to climb. . . . a slow, toilsome and very delicate journey. . . . Making his way to the edge of the ice, he at length found a place where a shoulder of a rock projected out . . . , and by a careful spring he crossed the gap.

Carefully choosing his route, Grinnell eventually climbed to the top of the saddle where he could see far to the west. The steep mountainside gave way to park-like country of open meadows and timbered streams below. Farther on, half hidden in the smoky haze from distant forest fires, he could see two deep canyons—one running northwest, the other southwest. "Far to the south stood a tremendous mountain, and in a great basin to the west of it lay a mighty mass of ice and snow—no doubt [another] glacier," he wrote in his diary. He had been looking down to Granite Park and into the McDonald Creek drainage, with Sperry Glacier to the south. The next day Grinnell and

Jack Monroe climbed to the saddle between Gould Mountain and Monroe Peak (now Angel Wing) to view the valley of Cataract Creek.

The hunters moved on to St. Mary Lake. Both Grinnell and North killed sheep on Singleshot Mountain; while carrying one of them back to the horses, Grinnell fell and wrenched his back—an injury that plagued him repeatedly thereafter. Undaunted, he scaled Otokomi and measured it with his barometer, registering 3,800 feet higher than St. Mary Lake (it is actually 3,451 higher).

The men also named the four prominent peaks south of St. Mary Lake. From northeast to southwest, they are: Red Eagle, for the Blackfeet medicine man who performed the Bear Pipe ceremony; Four Bears, for Joseph Kipp's grandfather, a Mandan painted by George Catlin in 1832 (in 1932 the mountain's name was changed to Four Bears' Mandan name, Matotopa); Little Chief, Luther North's Pawnee name; and finally, Almost-a-Dog, for the Blackfeet elder who tallied victims of the Starvation Winter.

An early November snowstorm drove the men back to the agency at Badger Creek. After meeting with the Blackfeet, Grinnell rode with Monroe and Gould to Great Falls and then continued toward home on the east-bound train.

The next year, 1889, Grinnell visited the Blackfeet Agency for only three days after spending some time with friends at Yellowstone and before hunting with Gould near Hope, British Columbia. Following a council with Bear Chief, White Calf, Running Crane, Many Tail Feathers and several others at the Two Medicine camp, he met and had a "good talk with Major Catlin," the new agent. For two years Grinnell had worked to get M. D. Baldwin, Catlin's predecessor, fired because of his dishonesty. His efforts received praise when the New York *Evening Post* printed "Three Letters" on July 31, 1889, from the Blackfeet to Fisher Cap (Grinnell) thanking him for his assistance. His concern for native Americans went beyond the Blackfeet, and later that year his first book, *Pawnee Hero Stories and Folk Tales,* was published by Charles Scribner's Sons.

In July 1890, Lt. George P. Ahern from Fort Shaw asked Grinnell about the feasibility of crossing the Continental Divide at the head of the Swiftcurrent. Grinnell believed it would be difficult to cross above its north fork, but offered the lieutenant precise directions for a possible route.

Though Grinnell had not yet explored the north fork of the Swiftcurrent, he planned to that autumn. He suggested to Gould that they first scout the Kennedy Creek drainage, then cross over to the Swiftcurrent and investigate its north fork while mapping the Continental Divide, and finally attempt to reach the headwaters of the St. Mary River by way of Cataract Creek.

To entice his companion, Grinnell suggested that afterwards they could float down the Missouri from Great Falls or Fort Benton and hunt in the badlands, hinting that his old pastime had not yet completely faded. Actually, he planned to visit the Arikaras on their Dakota reservation, spend a couple of weeks with the Pawnees, and stop by the Cheyenne, Arapahoe and Wichita agencies. He told Gould, "If I do all that and fill a lot of notebooks with this material, I think that I shall have done enough to satisfy me for the year 1890."

Grinnell met Jack Monroe on Kennedy Creek in early September; Gould arrived a week later. Wind and deep snow, combined with down timber and steep gulches, limited their exploration of Kennedy Creek. Instead of canvassing the countryside, they bagged a few blue grouse and sat around the campfire telling stories. Foul weather kept them from crossing through the mountains to the Swiftcurrent, so they descended Kennedy Creek and returned to Joe Butch Henkel's cabin near the Swiftcurrent's mouth, then proceeded upstream to the northern branch. In his diary, Grinnell described a unique sight:

> On the head of the fork . . . is a glacier, the foot of which is in a lake, below that is another lake, both blue. In the upper one this process of icebergs [calving is] exemplified by the foot of the glacier breaking off constantly and the lake being full of floating fragments of ice.

While going through some tangled timber Grinnell's horse fell, trapping the rider's leg against a log. In spite of his pain and lameness, he and Monroe climbed to a lofty point on Apikuni Mountain where they could see the headwaters of the Belly River and the valleys of both Kennedy and Swiftcurrent creeks, Cataract Canyon, and the St. Mary drainage. "A most superb prospect lay before us," Grinnell wrote in his diary:

> . . . Glaciers were on every Mt. almost. A number on the Mts. about head of St. Mary's were very large. One especially on S. Fork of St. Mary's covers the whole Mt., a very large one, from summit as far down as we could see it without a break. We call it the Blackfoot glacier and the Mt. the Blackfoot Mt.

He took bearings on several mountains—Chief, Gould, Grinnell, Wilbur, Going-to-the-Sun, Divide and Flattop—before returning to the agency and heading east.

Throughout the fall he visited the Plains Indian reservations, as he had planned, but he did not accomplish as much as he hoped

51

Iceberg Lake.

because of the widespread religious fervor over the Ghost Dance, a last-ditch and intense though short-lived hope among many Indians that their cultures and souls might be saved from the incursions of the whites. By the time Grinnell arrived in New York he had already decided that his goal for next year's trip would be to explore that huge glacier he had named Blackfoot.

Mapping the Continental Divide

By early 1891 the Blackfeet Reservation had yet another in its rapid succession of mostly corrupt agents. Maj. George Steell, however, apparently gained respect from Grinnell; despite that, during his watch over the agency he caught Jack Monroe selling whiskey and expelled him from the reservation. Pragmatic as ever, Grinnell told his mountain companion in a letter that spring: "I have not the slightest sympathy for your misfortune. . . . It would have been a great thing for you, if you could have made a few more trips over the mountains at the same profits that you made in the first two." Jack's banishment meant Grinnell would have to find someone else to accompany him on his autumn visit. He got Schultz to come along as cook and hired William "Billy" Jackson, a Blackfeet mixed blood, to climb with him and carry the camera.[16]

Grinnell had met Jackson the previous year and perhaps sixteen years earlier, when Billy served as a scout with Custer in 1874 on the Black Hills expedition. Two years later Jackson rode with Reno's contingent at the Little Big Horn, where, separated from the rest of the troops, he saw Charley Reynolds and Custer's chief scout Bloody Knife die. Later still he scouted for the Canadian government during the Riel Rebellion, after which he returned to the reservation and built a home on Cutbank Creek.

By the time Grinnell was ready to leave for the St. Mary country, he had enlisted two more companions: from Auburn, New York, came William H. Seward, Jr.—a young attorney, avid amateur photographer and grandson of Lincoln's secretary of state; and from Yale, Henry L. Stimson, a classmate of Seward's who had just passed the New York bar exam. Stimson went on to a distinguished career in public service as governor general of the Phillipines and President Hoover's secretary of state and secretary of war under Presidents (Franklin) Roosevelt and Truman.

In addition to his regular gear, Grinnell packed a surveyor's compass and a plane table. Although he still carried his rifle, he did not plan to use it; instead, he asked Schultz to take the young men hunting for sheep and goats so he would have more time for mapping.

Grinnell arrived at Billy Jackson's cabin a day ahead of Seward and Stimson. While they waited for the others, Joe Kipp introduced him to the sport of chasing coyotes with greyhounds. Once assembled, the five men headed for Henry Norris's cabin by the inlet to Lower St. Mary Lake. Though forest fires obscured the nearby mountains in a haze the party set out immediately along the west side of the upper lake, following an old Kootenai trail. On a narrow ledge at Goat Mountain they met with an accident. Grinnell described the event in his article, "Crown of the Continent":

> For a few yards below the crossing, the sharply sloping mountainside is overgrown with alders, and then breaks off in a cliff one hundred feet high. The trail is twelve or fifteen inches wide, but appears narrower. . . [Suddenly] they heard a yell of

dismay from the man in front, and then a shout: "The black mare has rolled down the hill!" Slipping off their horses and leaving them standing in the trail, they ran forward, and reached the scene of disaster just in time to see the second pack-horse spring upon a large flat rock which lay in the way, and as its four unshod feet came down on the smooth stone, it slipped, lost its footing, and rolled slowly off the trail. It had not fairly got started before the men had it by the head and had stopped its descent, holding it by the loosened hackamore. The animal made one or two struggles to regain its footing, but the brush, the slope and its

Sketch from "The Crown of the Continent" illustrating the fall of the black mare. —The Century Illustrated Monthly Magazine, September 1901

load made it impossible for it to rise, and it lay there while the three men held it. Meanwhile the black mare by a lucky chance had regained her feet before reaching the precipice, and was now making her way up the slope toward the trail.

They removed the pack from the horse, got it back on its feet and continued on to a camp where the damage could be repaired.

The next day they pushed on to the head of St. Mary Lake and set up camp. While Seward and Stimson hunted in the "Colonel's Basin" (Baring Creek) the following day, the others tried to force a trail up the St. Mary River. In his diary, Grinnell described the area as "absolutely virgin ground . . . no sign of previous passage by human beings; no choppings; no fires; no sign of horses." They took two days to travel the short distance; "nothing but Billy Jackson's good nature and my profanity pulled us through," he later explained to Gould.[17]

They started to climb around the point of a huge mountain on their left that Grinnell called Citadel. In a letter to Jack Monroe, he said:

> The timber was thick, and much of it down; lots of mire in the river bottom; plenty of rocks and willow and alder brush, as high as a horse's head, and so thick that often it was impossible to get an animal to face it until the man in the lead had gone ahead and either chopped out or broke down the way for them.

They were rewarded for their effort: a glimpse of their destination. Grinnell told Luther North, "Up on the head of the South Fork [of the St. Mary River] is the biggest glacier in the whole country and it runs down off what is about the biggest mountain." This was not Blackfoot Glacier, but another just to the west, and he named it and mountain for Billy Jackson. The two men climbed about on its slopes and took bearings while their young companions hunted. Seward, climbing up to a ledge, met face to face with a goat on its way down; both retreated.

Fog masked the glacier the next day, so Grinnell, Stimson and Schultz rode along the stream and found a small lake below a pass that looked like the rear sight of a rifle. They named the lake, pass and mountain to its north, Gunsight. Farther north they saw a tall, square-topped mountain and named it for *Forest and Stream* managing editor Charles B. Reynolds; another prominent mountain east of Blackfoot they called Mount Stimson. (This later became Mount Logan; Stimson was honored with another mountain to the south.) When they reached the top of the pass Grinnell realized he was on the Continental Divide.

In "Crown of the Continent," he wrote: "On the west side of this pass is another little lake, from which a stream runs southwest toward the Pacific Ocean. The wall of rock separating these two lakes is not more than one hundred yards in thickness, and to tunnel it would afford a passage for a railway with but slight grade." Grinnell may have said this merely to help readers visualize the geography; however, as a pragmatic man who had traveled across the Rocky Mountains on the Canadian Pacific Railroad, he may also have imagined genuine value in this idea, particularly after his recent struggle up the St. Mary River valley.

With enough provisions left for four more days, the group moved their camp up to Gunsight Lake. In the evening they spotted a number of goats high on the ledges north of the lake on a mountain they originally called Foresight. Stimson and Seward "fired fifteen or twenty shots a long range, but killed nothing." The goats, never having been shot at before and not understanding the noise or the poofs of dust from the bullets that struck near them, slowly climbed over the crest until the firing stopped, then returned. As a tribute to

The Grinnell party forces its way through the thick brush on the St. Mary River, 1891. From the "Crown of the Continent." —The Century Illustrated Monthly Magazine, September 1901

DRAWN BY W. H. DRAKE, FROM AUTHOR'S PHOTOGRAPH.

CUTTING A TRAIL THROUGH FALLEN TIMBER.

this unsuccessful barrage, Grinnell changed the name of the mountain to Fusillade.

The next day Grinnell and Jackson climbed Fusillade to chart the northern branch of the St. Mary River. Again rough and difficult country with thick fallen timber, steep slopes, snow slides and alder brush slowed their progress. At the summit they could see a park-like plateau extending from the foot of Mount Reynolds. To the north lay another imposing square-topped mountain, which they named Piegan Mountain, and farther to the north they correctly identified Mount Gould. Grinnell drew a sketch of the visible drainages and surrounding mountains.

By 4:30 P.M. they started down the mountain, but soon found themselves in "a perfect confusion of down timber, alders and vine brush," which they fought through until darkness forced them to spend the night on a level spot where they could tie their horses and build a fire. At daylight, they resumed their return to camp and soon reached it, tired and hungry, only to find that the horses in camp had eaten the baking powder; the sugar was gone, too, and only some flour and bacon remained. "Appekunny looks back on the trip with entire disgust for the reason that . . . we lived principally on mush and glaciers," he wrote Gould.

Vision of a Park

The trip back to Norris's cabin took two days. During that time Grinnell's patience with Stimson grew thin, prompting him to write in his diary: "I have not liked some remarks made by Stimson and shall let [him] go to Kootenai alone. . . . On strength of his few weeks spent in Colorado thinks that he 'knows it all.'" While the others went out to hunt, Grinnell stayed behind at the cabin to work on his map and notebook. On a page dated September 17, he wondered to himself:

> How would it do to start a movement to buy the St. Mary's Country, say 30 x 30 miles from the Piegan indians at a fair valuation and turn it into a National reservation or park. The Great Northern R.R. would probably back the scheme and T. C. Power would do all he could for it in the Senate. Mr. Noble might favor it and certainly all the Indians would like it. This is worth thinking of and writing about.

Grinnell and Henry Norris went up on Flattop the next day to trace the course of Boulder Creek and take bearings. From the summit, looking northwest, he saw Mount Wilbur, Apikuni Mountain, the valley of the Belly River and Mount Merritt; looking south, he identified Mount Jackson, Mount Stimson (Logan) and Blackfoot Mountain; Piegan Mountain rose in the west. While crossing some slide rock on the return trip, Grinnell's horse got the lead-rope of the pack horse under his tail and began to buck, then fell with the rope tangled in his legs. Grinnell jumped, landed on his head, then "turned about a dozen sommersaults." He cut his head, scraped one leg with the rope, and bruised the other.

In the following days the men paired off to hunt—Stimson with Jackson, Seward with Schultz. Norris and Grinnell rode up to Red Eagle Lake to take bearings and sketch all the visible drainages. With no scarcity of mountains, Grinnell named one on the Continental Divide for Norris. Stimson left for home a few days later; Seward, Schultz and Grinnell set out for the Swiftcurrent.

After setting up their camp below Swiftcurrent Falls, Grinnell and Seward hunted for goats on the large mountain south of their camp. Grinnell proposed naming this one after Seward, but the young man objected and suggested instead that they name it for his sister, Cornelia Allen, which they did.

When Seward finally spotted a goat, he fired eight shots before bringing it down—"a somewhat reckless expenditure of ammunition," his host observed. Meticulously, Grinnell used rocks to prop up the carcass in a life-like position, then piled more rocks on which to set Seward's camera so the background would show the stratified rock ledges. He later presented the photograph to F. M. True, a curator at the United States National Museum, as a model; True was building a diorama to display mountain goats but had never seen one alive.

The men spent the next day resting from the labor of carrying the meat back to camp "after having fallen down all the cliffs on Mount Allen, and having waded all the streams and swamps in Swift Current Valley, and having scratched off most of our skin and clothing, wandering around in the dark in burnt pine thickets." Snow too deep for travel kept them in camp listening to Billy Jackson tell Blackfoot stories.

When the weather improved, Schultz and Grinnell climbed Cataract Mountain, presumably to hunt, though Grinnell actually wanted to see if he could recognize any landmarks to the south; he identified the headwaters of the St. Mary River, Blackfoot Mountain, Citadel Mountain, Mount Jackson and a shoulder of Reynolds Mountain. Another day, Grinnell, Seward and Schultz climbed to the summit of Grinnell Mountain, where Seward shot a goat but could not recover it because it fell over a high cliff. They spent their last day on the

Swiftcurrent scaling Mount Allen. Grinnell frequently took bearings and discovered a remarkable hole at the head of Canyon Creek where lofty cliffs towered over a small glacier and narrow lake (later named Cracker). He called the glacier and mountain Siyeh, after a Blackfoot chief.

Back at Norris's cabin, the First Cavalry's C Company, commanded by Lt. W. C. Browne, had arrived from Fort Assinniboine. Browne had taken a detachment of ten men, eight pack horses and Henry Norris as a guide to explore the headwaters of the St. Mary River. Grinnell left a sketch map of the St. Mary valley with the lieutenant's soldiers. Browne's exaltation at penetrating an unknown region dimmed when he learned that Grinnell had just come from the same country.

By the time Browne returned to the cabin, Grinnell had already left to ride up Boulder Creek—the only drainage in the area he had not yet explored—and then went directly to the agency. Though he and Browne never met, they corresponded frequently over the next year and exchanged each other's maps. Grinnell made a number of suggestions about the location of features on Browne's map, particularly in the Swiftcurrent region. He believed, with typical humility, that Browne's labeling of Grinnell Mountain as "Swift Current Mountain" was "much better than the name of an individual," adding, "I have no ambition to see my name on the map." Nevertheless, when he suggested that Browne name a particular peak, the lieutenant chose Mount Merritt to honor Gen. Wesley Merritt, the military commandant of the Dakota region. He also substituted Grinnell's name on his map for Swiftcurrent Mountain.

In May 1892 Grinnell asked the editor of *Century* magazine if he would be interested in an article about the St. Mary country. "The scenery . . . is wonderfully grand; the mountains high and remarkably bold. . . . Some day it will be a great resort for travelers. . . . The mountains . . . lie within the boundary of one of the proposed forest reserves, and some day I hope may be set aside as a National Park. . . ." By November, the manscript had been completed and accepted by *Century*. He thought publication might be delayed until summer "since it deals with snow covered mountains." He never imagined that nine years would pass before the article appeared.

Little Dog, as spokesman, makes an offer for a land exchange with the commissioners.

VI

The Ceded Strip, 1895

W HITE INVASION OF THE ST. MARY REGION and Blackfeet country occurred relatively late compared to other parts of the West. Prior to the main surge of American western expansion, the Blackfeet had acquired horses and guns and had developed a reputation among the whites as a fierce people. Their legendary savagery helped them keep their northern plains homeland in modern Montana and Alberta largely free of intruders through the 1860s. But by early in 1870 disease, slaughter of buffalo herds and a malevolent massacre led by Maj. Eugene M. Baker had effectively neutralized the Blackfeet's ferocity.

Prospecting parties wasted no time penetrating the region: in 1870 the Frank Lehman party crossed Marias Pass from the west and searched for copper before moving on to Alberta; in 1876 a group of Texans under William Veach prospected around the St. Mary lakes and found a large gold nugget near Quartz Lake; and about four years later Henry A. Kennerly "washed for gold on Swift Current and Kennedy's Creek." Even James Willard Schultz in 1884 "picked up several pieces of float quartz, which were rich with gold and silver."

Rumors of Wealth

On January 25, 1894, acting Blackfeet agent Capt. Lorenzo Cooke addressed thirty-two influential members of the tribe. For the past two years, growing numbers of whites had been secretly prospecting in the mountains on the reservation's western edge. Each rumor spawned an increase in the value of the copper, silver and gold they said was "locked up" on the Indian land. Even the Blackfeet imagined their land worth more and more. News of these mineral finds in the St. Mary country disturbed George Bird Grinnell. "Paradise may soon be invaded by mines," he wrote George Gould that spring. But he doubted that any extremely valuable claims would be found, noting to Montana Senator T. C. Power: "I have been running around over those mountains for the last eight or ten years, and never saw any great sign of mineral."

Captain Cooke asked the tribal leaders to consider selling the mountains as a solution to the constant trespassing by the whites, assuring them that he "had no interest in their decision one way or another." After discussing the idea among themselves, the Indians wanted Grinnell and Charles E. Conrad, a Kalispell banker, to negotiate the sale on their behalf. Aware of his geological ignorance, Grinnell urged Interior Secretary Hoke Smith and the United States Geological Survey to send a mining expert who could evaluate the discoveries. If significant mineral wealth existed, Grinnell suggested the secretary appoint a commission to negotiate with the Blackfeet for the purchase of their land.

Seven years earlier, in 1887, the Blackfeet had signed a treaty relinquishing their lands north of the Missouri River and east of Cut Bank Creek—most of their reservation. For it, the tribe received $150,000 annually for ten years, which was supposed to produce economic independence and cultural assimilation by turning its members into ranchers and farmers. But a series of incompetent and inexperienced agents wasted, stole or swindled the money; this time both the Indians and Grinnell wanted a better plan. Grinnell did not know Captain Cooke, but the Indians complained that, while he seemed to be keeping other whites out, he sent his son and his own employees to prospect on the reservation.

Concerned with the welfare of the tribe as the final payments approached, Grinnell wrote Blackfeet agent Maj. George Steell in July that the Indians "will be in serious need of further aid. . . . Indians are not competent to meet white men in business. . . . " He rejected serving on a commission, adding, "The only motive that can influence me in this matter is the good of the Indians, and no other consideration can enter into my view of the case." Disappointment loomed: "I had hoped that it might be practicable to set off the mountain part of the Piegan reservation as a national park, or a forest reserve, but if minerals actually exist there, . . . there is of course no hope that my plan can be carried out."

In the fall of 1894, as Grinnell prepared to leave for the mountains to see the minerals and mines for himself, he realized this trip required additional preparation. "There are no picnickers in the country," he wrote Secretary Smith. "The discovery of the mines has resulted in a continuous chasing around by Indian police, who are active in driving white people out of the country." Grinnell asked the secretary for a letter granting him permission to travel inside the reservation and agreed to "look into matters with the Blackfeet."

Billy Jackson would again accompany Grinnell; Jack Monroe remained banished from the reservation for selling whiskey in 1891, but returned unbeknownst to his eastern companion later in 1894. Grinnell informed Jackson that after seeing the mines, he wanted to go "directly up the head of the river and try to climb the Blackfoot mountain." Just before leaving for Montana he discovered that *Century* magazine had his only map and obtained a copy.

Still reluctant to give up hope for a national park, he interrupted his journey in St. Paul to present in person the idea he had written about to F. J. Whitney of the Great Northern Railroad. Grinnell envisioned

> a public park and pleasure resort, somewhat in the nature of Yellowstone National Park, or the Banff National Park on the Canadian Pacific. I presume you are familiar with the St. Mary's Lakes. I am sure that Mr.[James J.] Hill [president of the Great Northern Railroad] is, for I remember a year or two ago having quite a long talk with him on this subject. The matter is one of great interest to me and to other men in the east, and it should be of interest to intelligent persons of Montana.

Three dozen Blackfeet friends welcomed Grinnell when he arrived at the site on Willow Creek where the new agency was still under construction. Though wanting to council with them, he was more anxious to travel the region he had not seen for three years. "These mountains are grand beyond words; I had forgotten their sublimity. They are truly sky reaching," he extolled in his diary.

Heavy rain and deep snow in the higher elevations prevented him and Jackson from climbing Blackfoot Mountain, so they headed north to the Swiftcurrent. At Henkel's cabin, Joe Butch enthusiastically predicted the local mines would "make a bigger camp than Butte." He and Jackson moved up to their usual camp below Swiftcurrent Falls. Unable to find the mines in the snow, they sat in their lodge and smoked and told stories. Henkel arrived the next day and showed them a prospect hole on the north fork. Grinnell took some ore samples from the dump and from three seams that looked rich in copper. Henkel said eight seams came together to form a main lead, eight to ten inches thick; Billy Jackson claimed even this was only a spur. Inclement weather forced them back to Henkel's place and then to the agency.

After "a long and tiresome council" with twenty-five to thirty Indians, during which he "tried to explain the bad things and praised the good," Grinnell and Captain Cooke drove over to Badger Creek to see the irrigation ditch the Indians were building under the supervision of Bureau of Reclamation engineers. Later, Grinnell told the Indians he was disappointed with the gains they had made toward assimilation. "White Calf made the same old tiresome kick and I had to shut him off as I also did Siyeh," he wrote in his diary.

The Commission

The Blackfeet, Grinnell reported to the interior secretary, were "making satisfactory progress toward civilization." Though they disliked the agent's military ways, Cooke encouraged them to take care of their cattle, prevented traders from cheating them, kept whites off their range and limited the whiskey trade. In his letter to Secretary Smith, Grinnell recommended increasing their beef issue by twenty-five percent and sending 3,000 cows with calves the next spring, along with three more threshing machines. (Instead of getting three threshers, the Indians got one so large and heavy that it was, for practical purposes, stationary.) Grinnell described to Smith the mineral leads he had seen and again asked the secretary to send a competent mining expert to evaluate the area.

Though prospectors continued to invade the Blackfeet Reservation, it had not reached the proportions that took place in 1893 farther east on the Fort Belknap Reservation. News of gold in a small stream on the southern slopes of the Little Rocky Mountains had created such a stampede of miners and stockmen that they formed a settlement there. By the fall of 1894, the illegal town called Landusky had, in addition to its ubiquitous saloons, a post office and regular stage service.

The Indians Appropriations Act of March 2, 1895, authorized the interior secretary to appoint a commission to negotiate with the Indians to sell the infringed portions of the Blackfeet and Fort Belknap reservations. His request that Grinnell serve on the commission was met with hesitation, then the suggestion that he would rather recommend others and participate only as an advisor. However, when the secretary sent a telegram asking him to reconsider, Grinnell accepted, deciding he might be able to do more for the Indians by being a member of the delegation. He gave Smith one last chance to change his mind by asking him whether the Interior

Department wanted the commission to drive a hard bargain or offer a fair price. "I assume," he wrote the secretary, "that you wish to have justice done in the matter."

Along with Grinnell, Smith appointed William C. Pollock of the Bureau of Indian Affairs and Walter M. Clements, a Georgia attorney, to the commission. Grinnell decided they should all spend two or three weeks on site in the mountains and asked Billy Jackson and Jack Monroe to meet them at the Blackfeet agency about the first of September. Pollock wanted to bring his wife, which suited Grinnell since he already planned to bring his brother Mort, whose wife had just died, in the hope that a trip west might help ease his brother's grief and loneliness.

On August 30, Grinnell and his brother boarded the train in Shelby, just east of the reservation, and found both Pollock and Clements there. The commissioners spent the following day observing distribution of government issues to the Indians at the agency. Maj. George Steell, along with Charles E. Conrad, A. B. Hamilton and Joseph Kipp, had already visited the Swiftcurrent with ten Piegans.

Joe Kipp.

"We saw very little, and in fact, did not try to see much," Steell noted in a letter to former agent Cooke.

The commissioners had barely arrived at the agency when an unruly horse upset the wagon in which they were riding. Clements fell out onto a pile of rocks and injured his knee, confining him to bed for the next three weeks. Meanwhile, Grinnell and Pollock held an informal council with about two hundred Indians on September 2. They selected four full bloods, four mixed bloods and Ross Cartee, the agency engineer, to accompany them to the lands in question early the next morning.

On the way to the Swiftcurrent brother Mort and Jack Monroe spotted a large female grizzly on a hillside above the trail and went after it. "She chased Jack up a tree, wounded both dogs and came near killing Jack. Mort shot her the last time and she fell at Jack's feet. Jack had fallen down, his gun wouldn't work—a most exciting and dangerous scrimmage," Grinnell observed in his diary.

They first visited the large lead at the base of Mount Wilbur near Bullhead Lake, then moved on toward Grinnell Glacier. A cold rain interrupted the investigation; some waited for the weather to clear while others went hunting. The next day, while one group examined a lead that passed through Mount Gould, Grinnell, Cartee, Monroe and three of the Indians rode up Cataract Creek and climbed to the summit to look down into the St. Mary valley. The bitter cold wind chilled Grinnell so deeply that he did not recover until he crawled into bed that night.

The party left for St. Mary Lake the next morning and reached Henry Norris's cabin after dark. Continued rain and wind made travel miserable, but Grinnell climbed to the top of East Flattop to take compass sightings. "I was never wetter in my life, . . . terrible rain and wallowing through wet brush," he logged in his diary on September 13: When the sky cleared, Grinnell, Monroe and Cartee climbed a shoulder of Little Chief to view Blackfoot Glacier and the valley of Virginia Creek.

Most of the group headed back to the agency on September 17, two weeks after their departure. Grinnell and Monroe remained an extra day to hunt on Divide Creek and visit Kootenai Lick, but they saw no game. When they finally returned to the agency, Indians flocked to Grinnell, each with a different story. "The whole thing is amusing but sickening," he noted in his diary, then added with empathy, "See both sides of the game."

Striking a Deal

On September 20, the commissioners met with the tribe, which asked for more time to select a committee of thirty-five to represent it. The next day Pollock explained that the Indian representatives' actions required approval by a majority of the male tribal adults. Grinnell and Clements assured the Indians that anyone could present an opinion and all would receive fair treatment from the commissioners.

The Indians argued over land values, but no one would suggest a fair price. "My eyes were long ago opened to the purposes of the Government," claimed White Calf, the tribal chief. "No other reservation has as valuable land as that which you came to buy." Three Suns submitted a different view: "We are to sell some land that is of little use to us. . . . If you wish to give a good price, we will be pleased."

On Cartee's map Pollock traced a north-northwest angling line from Two Medicine Creek near the railroad, through the inlet area between the upper and lower St. Mary lakes, on to Chief Mountain and finally due north to the Canadian border. White Calf wanted Cartee to alter the line so that the tribe would lose no prairie land. Little Bear Chief disagreed, reminding them that they were there to make a treaty and should do so immediately. He did not want to sell any timber or grazing land and suggested Cut Bank Creek be the southern border. He made an offer: "I would ask $2,000,000. When the Government has important transactions to make it sends smart men."

The meeting recessed so the Indians could resolve their differences and the commissioners could consider Little Bear Chief's proposal. When they reconvened, White Calf said the Indians agreed that Cut Bank Creek should be the southern boundary. Neither Grinnell nor Conrad offered any advice. Instead, faced with a proposal for a boundary that would not prevent white trespasses, Grinnell suggested postponing the proceedings until the commissioners could resolve that problem. Though he made no public comment, Grinnell noted in his diary that he told the Indians their asking price was absurd.

The Blackfeet delegation arrived at the Monday morning council almost two hours late. The disgusted commissioners admonished the Indians for their tardiness, adjourned without conducting any business, and rescheduled the meeting for 2 P.M. Little Dog appeared to be the new spokesman for the Blackfeet; he started by asking Pollock what they would offer for the land if the boundary was just north of the railroad. Until then, the commissioners had avoided quoting a price, but they had discussed it among themselves the day before. Pollock replied: "We have decided to propose to pay for the lands north from the railway $1,000,000, and from Birch Creek north $1,250,000."

Little Dog countered:

> I am about to make a proposition on that land and I think it will surprise you; make you faint and fall down. . . . We ask for the land north from the railroad $3,000,000, so we will be able to maintain ourselves and care for our wives and children. There are so many things in which the Great Father has cheated us. . . . Those mountains will never disappear. . . . This money will not last forever. I knew that you would be afraid when I told you our price.

Grinnell explained that Congress would have to approve the treaty, and this offer would make the Blackfeet look like fools. He said $1 million would allow the tribe to "grow fat and rich and your children to be happy"; however, if the tribe stood fast, the commissioners would have to leave and the Indians would gain nothing. "The Great Father told us to come here and treat with you. . . . If you don't want to trade with us, we must get on the train and go."

One after another, the Indians reaffirmed their position:

"I will not go out of the trail marked out by Little Dog," declared Little Plume.

"We are all willing to stand by him," said Three Suns. "We have set our price."

Middle Calf was firm: "We will not recede from our $3,000,000 offer."

Four Horns reminded the commissioners that the mountains contained the metal of watches—"something that is worth money."

"Open your ears," urged Yellow Wolf, "give us the $3,000,000 and we will all be happy."

Finally, Mad Wolf told the white men: "Now, you are going to decide what you will do. That is all."

Grinnell reminded the Blackfeet of his long association with them and said he would be lying if he led them to believe Congress would pay their price. "If you think the Government will make money by selling this land, you can let the Government take the land and sell it for you," he suggested. He still believed the land had little value in minerals and would not be purchased for settlement, so he recommended that the Indians take the $1 million.

Pollock suggested they meet again in the morning.

These Blackfeet Chiefs began negotiations for the "ceded strip" in 1892. Left to right: Running Crane, White Grass, Four Horns, Brocky, White Calf, Young Bear Chief, and Little Plume; Little Dog is seated in front of Brocky.
—J. N. Choate photo, Smithsonian Institution

"For what object shall we meet again?" asked Little Dog. "You have named your price and we have named ours. . . . Why meet again, then?"

"I am sorry we could not agree," answered Pollock. "We would willingly stay longer, but do not wish to urge you or force you to sell. The land is yours."

Almost as soon as the council adjourned the Indians were "sorry for their folly," Grinnell observed in his diary, "and desperately afraid lest we should go away."

Late that evening Major Steell and Joe Kipp persuaded the Indians to reconsider. The commissioners and the Indian representatives met again on Wednesday, September 25, and White Calf said his people would accept $1.5 million for the land under certain conditions. He said:

> Chief Mountain is my head. Now my head is cut off. The mountains have been my last refuge. We have been driven here and now we are settled. From Birch Creek to the [Canadian] boundary line is what I now give you. I want the timber because

in the future my children will need it. I also want the grazing land. I would like to have the right to hunt game and fish in the mountains. . . . We don't want our land allotted. . . . I shake hands with you because we have come to an agreement, but if you come for any more land we will have to send you away.

Pollock accepted the offer and read a treaty that he and Grinnell had drafted the day before, already aware of the Indians' change of heart.

Since payments would not begin until those under the previous treaty ended, in 1897, the banker Conrad suggested that interest be paid on the money in the interim. Pollock believed that the $250,000 over the commissioners' last offer took the place of interest. Conrad disagreed and told the Indians that the treaty was good, but they deserved to earn interest. "You have asked me to come and help you, to give you advice, and I want to do the same for you that I want any white man to do for me. . . . You must look out for your own interests. It is your right to do so."

Steell and Kipp joined Conrad in arguing for interest payments. The commissioners finally agreed and decided to increase the first year's payment to $300,000 instead of $150,000 and to allow four percent interest to accrue on money not spent from the annual disbursements.

"In the afternoon it [the treaty] was accepted and tonight everybody is glad," Grinnell wrote in his diary. "Many Indians made good speeches to me thanking me." He read the document to the council the next morning.

The treaty described a boundary line to be defined by an official survey. Indians would be allowed to cut timber for agency, school and personal use as long as the area remained as public lands. Montana game laws would govern the tribe's hunting and fishing rights. Indians would receive preference for agency jobs. Cattle issued for stock raising could not be sold or slaughtered and would be given preferentially, along with other goods, to those who showed appropriate industry and a willingness to lead a pastoral life. Rights for projects in the public interest, such as highways, railroads, telegraph and telephone lines, and irrigation canals, were granted. After the commissioners signed the document, the Indians began signing and continued for the next two days.

Their work finished, the commissioners boarded the train at Blackfoot and traveled to the Fort Belknap Reservation to complete their duties. Clements, ill with a cold and fearing he had pneumonia, remained on the train and returned to Georgia. After Grinnell and Pollock initiated their business at Fort Belknap, Pollock, too, became ill and was confined to bed. The remaining commissioner, Grinnell, borrowed a transit from a local engineer, surveyed the boundary and counciled with the Indians, who signed the treaty on October 9 and 10.

Back home in New York, Grinnell reviewed his efforts in the St. Mary country and wrote: "It grieved me to think of that beautiful country being defaced by civilization and improvements so called, but there seemed no way to avoid facing conditions which existed."

The rush is on—500 prospectors going for the gold—as Swiftcurrent Valley is officially open for miners in 1898.

VII

"The Crown of the Continent"

C ONGRESS RATIFIED THE TREATY that reduced the Blackfeet Reservation by redefining its western border on June 10, 1896, eight months after the Indians approved it, and specified that the land be surveyed before any settlement would be permitted in the "ceded strip." George Bird Grinnell—concerned about constant incursions by whites once they learned the government had purchased the land—urged that the survey be completed as soon as possible. He also worried about the impact prospectors and settlers might have on the watershed of the St. Mary country, source of both the Missouri and Saskatchewan rivers. Though the area contained little merchantable timber, fires started by the miners could destroy the small pines that helped retard erosion during the snow melt.

In December 1896 he asked Arnold Hague, an old friend and hunting companion at the United States Geological Survey, to persuade the Forestry Commission to incorporate this "important though not very extensive tract on the eastern flanks of the Rocky Mountains" in its forest reserve recommendations. Aware the commission was already considering a forest reserve between Lake McDonald and Flathead Lake, he suggested the St. Mary region be included as "an eastern extension of this larger reserve." Grinnell sent Hague a copy of his map showing the new western border of the Blackfeet Reservation and said, "The whole of this region ought to be protected." His friendship with Hague must have been efficacious: President Grover Cleveland's February 22 proclamation included

73

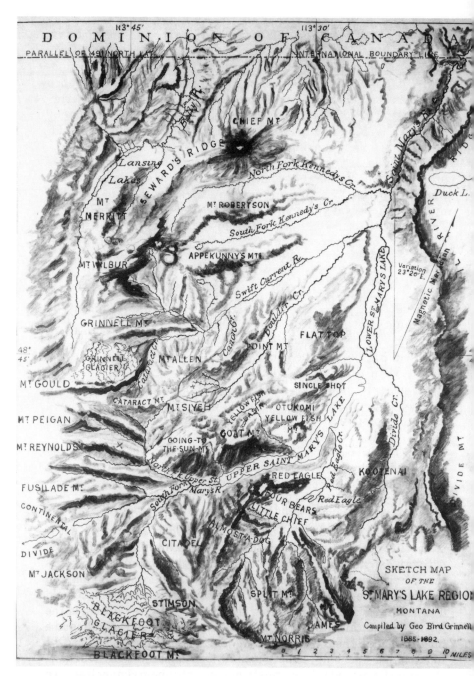

Grinnell's 1892 map, published in "The Crown of the Continent."

the ceded strip in the Lewis and Clark Forest Reserve, known today as the Kootenai, Blackfoot, Flathead, and Lewis and Clark national forests.

The government conducted its survey of the new Blackfeet boundary from the summer of 1896 to the summer of 1897, but did not open the area to miners and settlers until April 12, 1898. In the interim, sooners and squatters infiltrated the area in increasing numbers, keeping the Blackfeet police and military detachments from Ft. Assinniboine busy chasing trespassers.

Wild tales of rich mineral finds intensified gold fever among prospectors. Jack Monroe, who still occasionally supplemented his ranching income by smuggling whiskey, investigated mineral leads in the Swiftcurrent valley and offered to stake a claim for Grinnell. The idea of defacing this paradise disgusted Grinnell, who answered, "I should not care to take up a claim in the St. Mary's unless it positively threw itself in my face."

Climbing Mount Jackson

Since Grinnell missed his annual trip to the northern Rockies in 1896, he planned a spring outing in 1897 and looked for a guide. In a letter that April to his friend Emerson Hough, Grinnell said, "Jackson has always stood well up to the collar. . . . Schultz, of course, is not worth anything except as cook, and he irritates me even in that humble office." Jack Monroe's offer to supply two pack horses won him the assignment.

While crossing Reynolds Creek, the high water from the spring runoff swept them away. Grinnell later told George Gould:

> Jack lost his axe and the thumbnail of his right hand. I lost my gun, overcoat, various small articles of clothing, and for quite a long time my breath. For the rest of the day we were, of course, very wet, and matches and tobacco pretty well soaked, so that we could not smoke which was a deprivation.

In spite of the mishap, they succeeded in scaling Mount Jackson. After an early morning start, they reached the summit seven hours later. Far to the north a huge mountain rising from the northern drainage of the Belly River stood out higher than any others nearby. The two men discussed naming it. Grinnell said, " . . . that is the biggest mountain anywhere around here, and Cleveland is the biggest man in the country; let's call it Mt. Cleveland." Monroe, who liked the president, agreed: "Cleveland it is." On their return to camp, the climbers met a U.S.G.S. topographer with whom Grinnell shared his notes; the Geological Survey retained the mountain's name.

That fall Monroe guided Henry Stimson and Gifford Pinchot into the upper St. Mary drainage, intending to climb Blackfoot Mountain. Grinnell worried about this invasion of his private playground and asked Pinchot about the trip. "Blackfoot Mountain remains unconquered," Grinnell wrote with relief, "and until somebody goes up there I shall still regard myself as chief of the St. Mary's country." He began making plans to go back the next summer. "I shall not carry a gun, or even a fishing rod but shall take an alpine stock, and have a try at Blackfoot Mountain," he wrote Gould.

Grinnell arrived at the Blackfeet Reservation late in June 1898. After attending the Blackfeet Medicine Lodge, he and Jack Monroe packed into the head of the St. Mary River. They left their camp at the foot of Mount Jackson at 8 A.M. and crossed over the Blackfoot Glacier to a ridge on its northeast side, occasionally making long detours around crevasses. After scaling a twenty-five foot ice wall, they traversed a steep ice field using ropes and ice axes until they reached bare rocks. Reduced to crawling on their hands and knees for the last stretch, they finally crested the last ridge. In disbelief, Grinnell discovered a freshly overturned rock and feared they were not the first to reach the summit; closer inspection revealed it had been dislodged by a bear searching for food. The climbers spent three hours on the summit, taking compass readings and observing how Pumpelly Glacier attached to Blackfoot Glacier on its southeast side, then descended easily and rapidly returned to camp.

Boom and Bust

Earlier, in April, about five hundred prospectors raced up the Swiftcurrent valley when troops from Fort Assinniboine dropped the bars on the gate. Ten to twenty feet of snow at the heads of the streams delayed their staking claims, though a number of those previously located were promptly recorded in Choteau, the Teton County seat, 130 miles away. The Cracker claim at the south end of Cracker Lake and the Bull's Head on Mount Wilbur seemed the most promising, and both prompted wild expectations. Boomers offered $97.50 for Cracker Mine stock with a par value of $1 and were refused.

The town of Altyn, at the mouth of Canyon Creek, quickly rose from a tent city to a typical mining town, complete with false-fronted stores, a billiard parlor, two saloons and a dance hall. "Altyn will be one of two things," predicted the *Swift Current Courier*, "viz: the richest and biggest camp on earth or nothing. . . ." Little copper, and even less gold and silver, were found. By 1902 the boom turned to bust; miners, shopkeepers and Loun Sing, Altyn's laundryman, moved away.

Grinnell made his first contact with Montana Senator Thomas H. Carter in February 1899, in Washington, D.C., to discuss the management of the Blackfeet Indians and the appointment of a new agent. He told Schultz that Carter was "a great and good man for whom I have much respect. He was patient and polite, and I gave him my views with a certain amount of freedom." He sent the senator several letters and recommended several candidates for the agent position.

Grinnell did not return to the St. Mary country that year; instead he went to Alaska as a member of the Harriman Expedition. "I had a very delightful trip," he wrote a friend in September, proudly adding, ". . . [I] did not fire my rifle at any living thing." Occupied with Indian affairs and the publication of three books, Grinnell had little time to think about the St. Mary country at the turn of the century.

In March 1900, *Century* magazine informed Grinnell that his article, "The Crown of the Continent," written nearly eight years earlier, would soon be published. He had read little about affairs in the St. Mary country other than occasional newspaper reports on its copper mines, and he suspected that accounts lauding the richness of the operations were part of an overall "scheme to work off claims and stock on an innocent and confiding public." Meanwhile, continuing his conservation advocacy through articles in *Forest and Stream*, he urged the public to pressure Congress to establish another national park in the Appalachian Mountains and campaigned for creating game preserves within the forest reserves. He spent several weeks during the summer of 1901 studying the Blackfeet and Northern Cheyenne and returned home to find that *Century* magazine had published his article in its September issue.

Since Grinnell had been gone when the editor sent prepublication proofs, he did not get a chance to review the information. To make the article more timely, the *Century* magazine editor added a paragraph to the end of the article acknowledging the area's designation as part of the forest reserves in 1897. The map, he told Great Northern Railroad agent F. J. Whitney, "does not represent anything like the current state of my knowledge of the region, and is in some degree misleading." A bit dismayed by this inaccuracy but pleased by the compliments he received from several friends, he prepared for his first trip to the St. Mary country in three years.

Grinnell's cousin Ashbel Barney and brother-in-law Newell Martin accompanied him; Jack Monroe joined them as guide and compan-

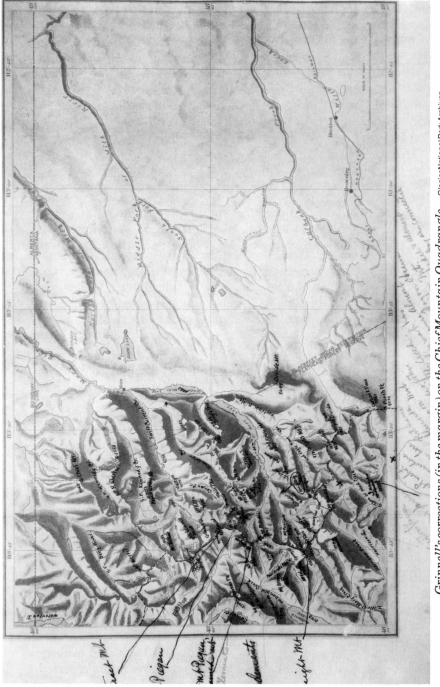

Grinnell's corrections (in the margin) on the Chief Mountain Quadrangle. —Glacier National Park Archives

ion. They camped at the base of Mount Jackson and tried to climb Mount Stimson (now Mount Logan), but found the way blocked by ice. While Barney and Monroe hunted goats, Grinnell and Martin rode up to Gunsight Pass to view the area west of the divide. Grinnell tried to orient himself based on a description of the area he had received from Professor Lyman Sperry. Sperry had climbed to Avalanche Lake in 1895 and to the glacier named for him the following year. Grinnell recorded in his diary on October 17, 1901:

> The valley on the other side is filled almost by a large rectangular lake. . . . mts on N & S of lake come down to water's edge. Rough jagged mts extend out from Jackson and Fusillade on N & S of valley. On N side, one a little back from valley had a snow cap with cornice. . . . Write Geol. Survey people. . . . Look up Sperry's description of Avalanche Basin. Jack is clear that this is A. basin.

Later they climbed Hairy Cap, the low shoulder between Fusillade and Reynolds where Barney killed a goat and Grinnell identified the pass between Piegan and Reynolds—he doubted a trail passed over it because of the steep walls. From vantage points, he could see Mounts Cleveland, Merritt, Grinnell, Gould, Pollock, Allen, Siyeh and Going-to-the-Sun, and, 125 miles to the east, the Sweet Grass Hills. On the way down they discovered twin lakes in the valley between Fusillade and Hairy Cap. Threatening weather sent them from the mountains to the inlet where the tiny town of St. Mary had sprouted during the prospecting boom.

On their way up the Swiftcurrent they passed by Altyn, which Grinnell described in his diary as "a dead camp." Other signs of civilization such as buildings, prospect holes and stumps dotted the landscape, but Grinnell found comfort in the things that remained as he knew them: ". . . Mtns. and my ice as beautiful as ever."

Early the next morning he and Martin climbed to Grinnell Glacier, passed over the west arm to the low sag in the Divide, then moved south on the west side of the Garden Wall to the base of Mount Gould. Ascending its west slope, they reached the summit about 7 P.M. After building a small monument of rocks, they headed back toward camp with only the moon to light their way. When the moon set, about 3 A.M., they had just reached a series of tangled ledges about a mile from camp. Unable to see through the black of night, they built a small fire, waited for daylight and finally arrived back in camp at 8 A.M. "I confess that I was tired," he recorded.

Grinnell discovered numerous signs that his treasured country had been pillaged by the influx of whites in recent years and reported to the chief forester, Gifford Pinchot:

On Swift Current I noticed that while a great deal of green timber had been felled, presumably for legitimate purposes, the tops were lying about unburned, and a good portion of the forest between the head of McDermott's Lake—the lake above Swift Current Falls—and the lower lake on my stream was in such a condition that the careless throwing down of a match or a cigarette might have burned up the whole country. I also noted that a very considerable number of fine straight green trees had been systematically peeled apparently in order to kill them. I imagine that dry timber may be cut without a permit, and I rather took it for granted that these trees had been girdled in order to make them dry in the course of the next two or three years. The mines on Swift Current seem to be in a most discouraging condition and the town is moribund, for all of which some people are duly grateful.[18]

Elizabeth

These two discoveries—the impending destruction of the St. Mary watershed by settlement and the collapse of the mineral exploration—reawakened Grinnell's desire for a national park. Further, the publication of "The Crown of the Continent" brought him a new ally, Francois E. Matthes, a topographer in the United States Geological Survey. Matthes and his associate, Bailey Willis, had surveyed the region in 1901; impressed with its natural beauty, they recommended preserving the area as a national park. Through the winter Grinnell and Matthes exchanged and compared notes on their respective maps.

Meanwhile, Grinnell encountered another distraction: "I have not been engaging a cook. . . . Time is sliding swiftly by and the days are coming when cooks may decline to be engaged by you and me . . . ," he wrote to George Gould. In another letter, the discussion continued:

> . . . I cannot agree with you on the question of cooks. It is true that devotion to the battle may often postpone the need of a cook, but inevitably the day comes when the battle ceases to cheer or even inebriate. When that time arrives, the system calls loudly for a cook. . . . You are perhaps too young to realize its truth, but I who have lived longer have my weather eye wide open for a cook.

Grinnell's "weather eye" landed on Elizabeth Curtis Williams, a twenty-four year-old widow who was interested in photography. Elizabeth had been attracted to Grinnell since September 1892, when, at the age of fourteen, she read an article he wrote for

Scribner's Magazine called "The Last of the Buffalo." In the spring of 1902 she volunteered to go with him to the Southern Cheyenne Reservation in Oklahoma Territory. He planned to use her photographs to chronicle ordinary Indian life in his book about the Cheyennes. He joined Elizabeth in Oklahoma in June after a slight delay while he looked into grazing leases at Standing Rock Reservation for President Roosevelt. Their work in Oklahoma completed, they returned to New York City in mid-July and were married a month later.[19]

In the summer of 1903 Grinnell took his young bride to the St. Mary country. After attending the Blackfeet Medicine Lodge on the Fourth of July, they headed for Kennedy Creek with Jack Monroe and another couple, Mr. and Mrs. John White. Grinnell lost little time in initiating Elizabeth to mountain climbing as they set out to conquer Chief Mountain. He wrote:

The Grinnell camp at the base of Chief Mountain. —Glacier National Park archives

We started at 7:30 and . . . rode to back of Mt. as far as horses could go. Then up slide rock to comb . . . reached summit after some labor. . . . The women climbed with extraordinary pluck and facility. At the very first they had a little difficulty, but in a very few minutes Elizabeth came to understand how to walk and balance.

Later, influenced by emotions softer than the mountains of rock, the infatuated groom wrote about the mountain flowers:

The grass we call soap grass is here called pine grass or sneeze grass. It has a tall flower stalk bearing a very delicate large oval blossom 8 in. high and two or three in diameter. Often when

George Bird Grinnell on Grinnell Glacier.

horses enter a patch of these blossoms—it flowers in July—they begin to snort and sneeze; hence the name. Saw a beautiful small purple clementis; it grows high up. The dogtooth violets have instead of a big single flower on a stalk . . . two, three and sometimes even four blossoms. . . . There are three columbines, a yellow, a white and a purple. . . . Yellow violets abound.

The party moved up the Swiftcurrent and camped below the falls, then climbed to Swiftcurrent Pass and along the Garden Wall to a point above Grinnell Glacier. "The way was long and hard. The women did splendidly," Grinnell wrote in his diary, never realizing that Elizabeth feared heights. She later confessed that she shivered with fear in the library of their home each year as she contemplated the high, narrow trails that awaited her next visit west. Such terror led to Elizabeth's frequent illness in camp. Still, she delighted in the wild beauty and freedom of the St. Mary country and almost always accompanied her husband, looking forward to the excursions with the sense "that nobody else had ever seen these things before."

The Early Campaign

Back in the office of *Forest and Stream*, Grinnell found his business manager, Edward Wilbur, seriously ill and his managing editor, Charles Reynolds, away for the spring and summer of 1904. Their absences dictated that he remain in New York. "Sometimes I feel as if I should like to drop work for two or three months and simply go off to the Rockies and loaf and camp until I was tired of it," he confessed to a friend.

Confined to New York, Grinnell occupied himself with thoughts of the St. Mary country. *Appalachia*, the journal of the Appalachian Mountain Club, published Francois Matthes's article, "The Alps of Montana," in April 1904—the same time that Grinnell received a copy of the new quadrangle map of Chief Mountain. He was delighted to learn that the Appalachian Mountain Club was interested in creating a national park in the Montana Rockies. "I should be very glad to do anything that I could to help forward a project to make a national park of any part of the region," he wrote Matthes.

A new obstacle appeared: oil was discovered in 1902 near Kintla Lake, and two years later the owner of the Altyn hotel reported traces of crude in his mine shaft. The oil boom was on! Prospectors staked claims all along the floor of the Swiftcurrent valley from the falls to the St. Mary River. Three drills were at work, with three more planned. "Everyone has a pocketful of certificates of oil stock . . . ,"

Grinnell observed in a letter to James Willard Schultz. "I believe this oil excitement will pass as the copper passed," he added, hopefully.

In spite of the petroleum speculation, Grinnell launched his campaign to promote a national park in the St. Mary country in 1905. He failed to persuade Senator Carter to introduce a bill to create a park, so he turned to friends in Montana and urged them to write to the senator. Like a good politician, Carter promised constituent John Losekamp in an August 1905 letter that he would "be glad to take the matter up on my arrival in the east with our mutual friend Mr. George Bird Grinnell and trust that some good may come of the conference." That fall, Grinnell began to use the pages of *Forest and Stream* to push actively for a national park in northwestern Montana:

> Still another country—practically without inhabitants—yet marvelous in its wonderful beauty and grandeur—is that known as the St. Mary's country. . . . It is a region of marvelous lakes, towering peaks, vast glaciers and deep, narrow fiords. Few people know these wonderful mountains, yet no one who goes there but comes away filled with enthusiasm for their wild and singular beauty.

The Great Falls *Tribune*, noting Grinnell's editorials, supported the proposal. With the public now generally favoring forest reserves and national parks, it stated on October 30, "it would not be so much of a task" to preserve both the grand scenery and the valuable watersheds and local citizens must take the initiative. "That is a hint that should not be lost on the people of the Flathead valley, Teton county and northern Montana. If they stir actively . . . they will receive the powerful support of the president, . . . Mr. J. J. Hill and the Great Northern Railroad."

But nothing happened, so in May 1906 Grinnell asked Matthes if he had made any progress. "I have not succeeded in achieving anything with regard to the proposed National Park in the Montana Rockies, and there is no bill to be introduced for it . . . ," Matthes replied. He had, however, aroused interest among the members of the Appalachian Mountain Club and suggested Grinnell contact them. Since he had no Montana map, he drew no boundary lines, but he suggested some possible borders to Grinnell:

> . . . the southern boundary [should be] . . . just north of the Great Northern. . . . The west boundary was to start . . . near the mouth of McDonald Creek in a N.W. direction along the foot of the main scarp on the east side of the valley of the North Fork of the Flathead, . . . a straight line . . . parallel to the Blackfoot

boundary. The Park proposed would contain roughly 1500 sq. miles, containing upward of 50 ice-bodies and over 200 lakes. It might fitly be called Glacier Park.

Grinnell assured Matthes that the oil boom had come to nothing— "hundreds of oil claims have been staked out . . . [but] not one pint of oil has been taken from the ground." He contacted the secretary of the Appalachian Mountain Club, Rosewell B. Lawrence, and offered information about the St. Mary region. Matthes agreed to mark the boundaries on a map and draw up a bill for a national park. Grinnell suggested to Lawrence:

> I am reasonably confident that we can get a Montana member of Congress to introduce the bill, preferably in the Senate. . . . I may say that Gifford Pinchot, United States Forester, and I believe President Roosevelt, will be heartily in favor of the establishment of such a Park.

Grinnell forwarded a land survey map of Montana to Matthes, not realizing there were many more chasms to cross and cliffs to climb.

President Taft signing Glacier National Park bill into law—April 11, 1910.

VIII

An Uphill Push, 1906-1910

E LIZABETH AND GEORGE BIRD GRINNELL visited the Northern Cheyenne Reservation in September 1906 before traveling on to the Blackfeet country. The Blackfeet were "faithfully striving to follow the white man's road"—striking for higher wages, Grinnell noted in his diary. The United States Bureau of Reclamation had hired the Indians to build a large irrigation ditch between the St. Mary and Milk rivers, but the workmen felt their compensation was too low. Grinnell spoke with the Indian leaders, then wrested a promise of higher pay from bureau engineer Cyrus Babb. The dispute settled, he and Elizabeth moved on to the narrows of St. Mary Lake and camped on Rose Creek.

Still unaware of the effect the mountains had on his wife, Grinnell noted in his daily journal, "E. has been quite ill with indigestion . . . , probably knocks out the trip." Rain and fog the following day further dampened Elizabeth's enthusiasm, so they left the St. Mary region and visited the Blood Reservation in Alberta, then crossed Crowsnest Pass and went up Kootenay and Arrow lakes to Revelstoke. Finally, they departed for home on the eastbound Canadian Pacific.

Grinnell was astonished at the changes that had taken place in Alberta since his first visit in 1887 and described them in a letter to George Gould: "People are raising wheat there, on the prairie mind you, and making a fortune. Cardstone [*sic*] . . . has a good steam heated electric lighted hotel—what do you think of a migration to Abyssinia, or to the mountains of the moon?"

Others were also sensitive to the changes taking place across the region; rumors circulating in the Flathead valley throughout 1907 prompted protests over the possibility that Lake McDonald would be included in a new national park. "There may be some local people who favor the park plan, but we have observed only two," noted the Kalispell *Inter Lake* late in September. Many residents, especially those who vacationed near the lake, believed the area was best served by remaining a national forest that allowed settlement. Although the concept of preservation seemed important, the development of prom-

The Grinnells in front of a Blackfoot lodge, their home when visiting the reservation. —Glacier National Park archives

ising oil discoveries around Kintla Lake offered an economic reason to oppose national park status.

The Great Falls *Tribune* criticized the *Inter Lake* for its narrow view: a few might enjoy the forest by obtaining land for a summer home, but

> . . . ten thousand would find enjoyment . . . if good roads were built and the scenery made accessible at a moderate cost. . . . The country belongs to all the people of the United States, and . . . patriotism and citizenship should dictate a policy that would make the country accessible and available to the most people. A national park would undoubtedly serve that end.

The *Tribune* emphasized the economic benefits to the town of Kalispell, area farmers and businessmen all along the Great Northern route. Great Falls expected to prosper as a "sort of half way station" between the new park and Yellowstone National Park. The paper urged Flathead valley residents to endorse the project and predicted they would be "well satisfied with their action in the future."

Early Legislation

The obstructionists' arguments intensified after Senator Thomas Carter introduced a bill on December 11, 1907, proposing the creation of Glacier National Park. The Kalispell *Journal* opposed the removal of harvestable timber from the market; the Whitefish *Pilot* spoke against the loss of good hunting grounds; and the Kalispell *Bee* wanted previously surveyed lands excluded from the proposed park. The *Inter Lake* repeated its earlier arguments and added that a national park would dash the Canadian Pacific's plan to connect its railroad to Kalispell through the North Fork of the Flathead River.

A prominent Kalispell attorney, Sidney M. Logan, offered his views to Senator Carter in a letter published in the *Inter Lake*. He claimed the benefits of a national park to the people of the United States would not be commensurate to the injustice done to the residents of Flathead County. He cited the loss of possible valuable minerals and feared the military would control this park as it did Yellowstone. Carter's reply pointed out that geological surveys had found no significant mineral deposits and indicated that the park would be managed with the "sympathetic touch of forest rangers" under the Department of Agriculture. Letters opposing the park or suggesting modifications of the bill poured into Carter's office.

Carter's original bill simply outlined the boundaries of the proposed park: the western border followed section lines in a stair-step configuration; the Middle Fork of the Flathead River marked the southern boundary; the eastern line paralleled the Blackfeet Reservation; and the international boundary formed the northern limits.

Because of the many objections he received, Carter revised his proposal and introduced a new bill on February 24, 1908. More specific and liberal than the first bill, this one provided for rights of entrance and exit to legitimately settled lands and mining claims and allowed leases for summer cottages. The proposed western boundary would follow section lines between surveyed and unsurveyed lands until it reached the North Fork of the Flathead River. Surveyed lands were thus excluded from the park and reserved for settlement.

A week before Carter introduced this measure, Grinnell wrote to him and asked for a copy of the bill. The proposed boundary, which included the best natural features and protected the major watersheds, pleased Grinnell. He was even more enthusiastic that Carter had initiated legislation and applauded the senator in another letter thanking him for his cooperation: ". . . this action of yours will be heartily approved by the citizens of Montana . . . and by a large number of people . . . who have been fortunate enough to visit the territory."

Grinnell had not remained idle while observing the congressional process. He contacted the secretary of the Boone and Crockett Club, Madison Grant, to solicit support for the bill from its executive committee. He also drafted a resolution for the club (see Appendix A) and forwarded it to Grant, requesting that a copy be sent to Carter. Since Grinnell could not attend the club's annual meeting the following month in Washington, D. C., he asked Grant to present it to the membership. In addition, Grinnell contacted Gifford Pinchot and other Boone and Crockett members familiar with the St. Mary country and asked them "to tell the Club something about why Senator Carter's bill should pass."

Grinnell continued his campaign through March 1908 with requests for support to every possible ally, including the Appalachian Mountain Club, sportsmen who knew something about the area, friends in Montana and an editorial in *Forest and Stream*:

> I have been trying to get Senator Carter to introduce this bill for a good many years, and at last he has done it. I want now, if I can, to arouse in his mind sufficient interest in his own bill to get him to push it to a vote. . . . A generation hence it will be as great a resort as is the Yellowstone Park.

This drive uncovered an unexpected supporter; Carter's wife had visited the St. Mary lakes and was enthusiastic about the area's

90

scenery. "The bill ought to have a potent ally in her," he observed in a letter to a friend at the Crow Agency.

The Senate Committee on Public Lands, where Montana's Senator Joseph Dixon managed the bill, made some alterations. It changed the proposed western border to the North Fork of the Flathead River, believing a natural line would cause less confusion in patrolling for game violations, and added a clause permitting Interior Secretary James Garfield to authorize the construction of a railroad along the North Fork. Garfield, however, recommended that park jurisdiction remain under the Department of Agriculture so that mature timber could be harvested to improve the forests. Agriculture Secretary James Wilson took a more utilitarian stance and recommended cutting timber from areas planned as hydro-power reservoirs; further, he endorsed allowing the Canadian Pacific to build a rail route through either Kishenehn or Starvation creeks in the northwestern corner.

The amended bill, along with the secretaries' comments and a description of the area from the United States Geological Survey, passed in the Senate without debate on May 15, 1908, and went to the House of Representatives the following day. The House Committee on Public Lands, chaired by Montana's Congressman Charles N. Pray, changed the jurisdiction of the park from the secretary of agriculture to the secretary of interior and removed the clause allowing railroad access to the North Fork, then recommended that the bill be passed.

Just as the bill entered the House for consideration, Grinnell left New York to spend the summer in Oklahoma studying the Cheyennes on their southern reservation. When he returned home, he learned the House of Representatives, for no apparent reason, had neglected to pass the bill. Bailey Willis of the Geological Survey suggested Grinnell seek help from the Great Northern Railroad district agent in Philadelphia, A. C. Harvey, who had spoken hopefully to Willis about the House passing the bill. Harvey's reply to Grinnell turned his request for help back to where it started; after noting that Carter had assured him the bill would go through the House, Harvey advised Grinnell, "If you have any influence with House members, I wish you would bring it to bear."

Grinnell could have appealed directly to the congressmen, but he had been reluctant to use that approach. Over twenty years earlier, while working on a bill to protect Yellowstone Park, he had told Luther North:

> Lobbying is the meanest work I ever did—I would rather break
> broncos for a living than talk to Congressman about a bill. It
> makes me feel like a *detested* pickpocket to do it. And then—after
> having undergone this shame—to find that after all the bill for
> which you worked will fail.

Instead, Grinnell again turned to the comfortable vehicle of *Forest
and Stream* with a series of articles that appeared late in 1908 and
in early 1909. He described the St. Mary lakes and the Swiftcurrent
region, pictured the area's mountains, streams and lakes, detailed
the birds and game, reviewed the history of the mineral exploration
period, and reminded his readers that he had been telling them about
the region for the past twenty-four years, concluding ". . . it is of the
highest importance . . . that the bill should pass."

Local opposition in Montana metamorphosed between the introduction of the first and second bills with many of the objections
satisfied by the latter. On February 1, 1909, the *Inter Lake* began
directing its concerns to the "throngs of wandering tourists" who
would invade the proposed park. "Extracting the dollars is apparently much more to the point than keeping a wilderness unspoiled for
a few nature lovers," it declared. The Great Falls *Tribune* countered
that the people of Flathead county would one day view the passage
of the bill "as one of the most beneficent acts of the present
congress. . . . In many ways it is far more attractive as a pleasure
resort than Yellowstone National Park."

The House finally passed the bill in a slightly different form. In
spite of local support and encouragement from sportsmen and conservationists, the Senate and House did not try to reconcile the bill's
differences and it died with the end of the Sixtieth Congress. Even so,
Grinnell remained hopeful and wrote in *Forest and Stream* that
April: "No doubt it will be reintroduced in the next Congress, and will
finally be enacted." In addition, Canada now seemed willing to set
aside an adjacent tract on the other side of the boundary, prompting
him to add:

> It is gratifying to see the readiness with which Canada appears
> disposed to co-operate with the United States in the work of
> conserving the natural things of this continent. Two such good
> neighbors may wisely work together for so good an object.

A *Third Bill*

Carter introduced a third bill to create Glacier National Park on
June 26, 1909, and it was promptly referred to the Committee on
Public Lands under Senator Dixon. This bill encompassed all the

previous suggestions and amendments, providing that the western border would be the North Fork of the Flathead River; valid existing property claims would be protected; mature, dead or down timber could be harvested; and the interior secretary could execute leases for parcels of ground for buildings to accommodate visitors.[20]

That August Grinnell again directed his attention to the region. He had not visited it for three years and wrote George Gould, asking him to accompany him but knowing he would be turned down.

> The trip will be one for invalids, children and weak women, and there will not be excitement enough in it to appeal to you. I shall like, if I can, to see once more the snow capped mountains, and craggy peaks of the upper lake and river, but I shall hardly be in shape to climb either for the mountain's scalp, or for that of any animal making its home high up among the rocks.

Once the Grinnells set up camp on St. Mary Lake below Baring Creek, Elizabeth, the embodiment of "weak women," became ill. Grinnell wanted to continue but could not: "E. sick in the night. This is the third night she has been sick and for the three I have had no sleep," he wrote in his notebook on September 18. Two days later, on their way back to the agency, he softened: "E. happened to remember my birthday."

In December he contacted Senator Carter to check on the status of the Glacier Park bill and found it was still in the Senate Committee on Public Lands. He urged Carter to push for its passage: "I know of no opposition to the bill, and there is certainly a strong feeling in its favor in Montana." On January 20, 1910, the committee amended the bill to allow for a railroad right of way along the North Fork of the Flathead River. Before passing the measure and forwarding it to the House on February 9, the Senate added provisions for the Reclamation Service to utilize water flowing from the area.

A month later Grinnell asked readers of *Forest and Stream* to write Congressman Pray, urging a speedy vote. "Let everyone now put his shoulder to the wheel and push." At the same time, he censured San Franciscans for advocating a dam that would flood the Hetch Hetchy valley to provide the city with water; he felt that national park lands should never be diverted to the use of a special group. He sent Pray a lengthy letter, explaining his concern for the Glacier Park bill:

> The establishment of this Park will, I believe, be a great thing for the state. Its great natural beauty will attract . . . a multitude of visitors, while the vast quantities of water . . . will in time benefit a great population living on the arid plains to the east and to the west. I venture to hope that you will do everything in your power to bring this bill to an early vote.

Because the Great Northern Railroad provided easy access to the region, historians as a group have assumed that it played a major role in the creation of Glacier National Park. Instead, Louis W. Hill, who became president of the railroad after his father retired, and other Great Northern officials maintained low profiles and participated in only minor ways during the establishment of Glacier National Park. During the congressional deliberations, though the railroad monitored the legislation, it concerned itself primarily with projects that covered its operational costs and produced its profits: irrigation projects in North Dakota, townsite and homestead developments in central Montana, and shipping produce from orchards in Washington State.

The railroad's involvement remained low key after Carter introduced his third bill in June 1909; however, in March 1910, just when Grinnell became alarmed because the bill appeared to be stalled in the House Committee on Public Lands, the railroad stirred. Hill's private secretary sent him a telegram considered sensitive enough to deserve coding:

HAVE LETTER FROM SENATOR CARTER TO EFFECT GRANARY [GLACIER] PEDIGREE [PARK] BLUNDER [BILL] SURGEON [STUCK] INDELIBLE [IN] PYTHON [PUBLIC] LEAVENINGS [LAND] COMMITTEE OF HOUSE ASKS IF YOU CAN TAKE UP WITH CONGRESSMAN [Asle J.] GRONNA OF NORTH DAKOTA [Andrew J.] VOLSTEAD OF MINNESOTA AND [William W.] MCCREDIE OF WASHINGTON WHO ARE ON COMMITTEE MR [L. C.] GILMAN WILL TAKE UP WITH MCCREDIE DO YOU WISH TO WIRE OTHERS

Hill wired Gronna and Volstead at the same time that Grinnell contacted Pray and other Congressmen. Pray informed Grinnell that the bill, with amendments, had been reported out of committee to the House on March 15. Nothing more was heard from the Great Northern Railroad.[21]

A blizzard of letters flew from Grinnell to friends, Boone and Crockett Club members and congressmen. Using any angle to his advantage, he reminded his own congressman, William S. Bennett, "that my old friend Mr. Stiles, your uncle, went through that region something like forty years ago with Prof. Pumpelly," and suggested that Stiles, *if still alive*, would be enthusiastic about the bill. He wrote popular magazines such as *Century* and *Outlook*, asking for "a favorable word." He drafted a letter for the Boone and Crockett Club's game committee to send to influential citizens throughout the United States; he even suggested that the club offer associate membership to Senators Carter and Dixon.

94

To Grinnell's delight, the House passed the bill on April 13. He sent congratulations to both Carter and Pray and celebrated this advance with an editorial in *Forest and Stream*, writing: ". . . We believe that the day is not distant when great crowds of tourists will visit this wonderful region." Even though this multitude of tourists would need accommodations, Grinnell fought off suggestions that an appropriation needed to be appended to the bill. He wanted nothing to interfere with the bill's passage and asked his friends to reassure the chairman of the House Appropriations Committee.[22]

Senator Dixon informed Grinnell at the annual Boone and Crockett dinner two weeks later that the Conference Committee had agreed on the bill after the House deleted its amendment preventing railroads and the Bureau of Reclamation from entering the park. After the Senate and House accepted the Conference Committee report on May 4, Pray telegraphed the news to Grinnell. A temporary absence of President William Howard Taft from Washington worried him and he wrote J. Walter Wood that day, "I shall be a little bit easier in my mind when I learn that the President has signed the Glacier National Park Bill."

While Grinnell waited, Edward VII died in England and Halley's Comet delighted thousands of nocturnal viewers. Taft finally returned to Washington and signed the Glacier National Park Bill into law on May 11, 1910. In *Forest and Stream* ten days later, Grinnell thanked Carter, Dixon, Pray and the Boone and Crockett Club but took no credit for himself:

> To receive credit for good work well done is pleasant but a reward far higher . . . comes from the consciousness of having served the public well. . . .

Both Congressman Pray and Senator Carter sent letters congratulating Grinnell and thanking him for his efforts. No one acknowledged Louis W. Hill.

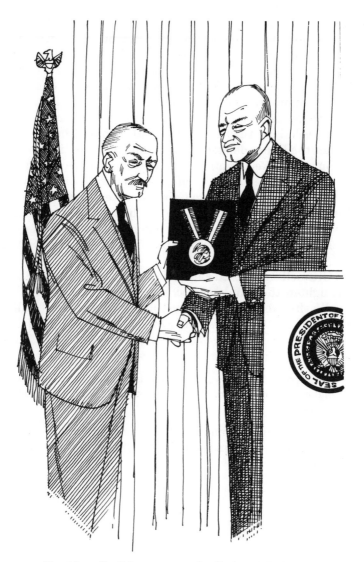

President Coolidge presents the distinguished service medal to George B. Grinnell, age 76, April 1925.

IX

Reluctant Hero

I N THE SUMMER OF 1911 crews readied Glacier National Park for the expected tourists. Though limited by a congressional appropriation of only $15,000, workers cleared the right of way for a twenty-four-foot wide paved road from Belton (West Glacier) to Lake McDonald and widened trails to eight feet along the St. Mary River and Swiftcurrent, Red Eagle and Cut Bank creeks. Even with work slowed by heavy spring rains, park Superintendent William R. Logan had told George Bird Grinnell in a letter on May 23 that he hoped to have all the trails in good shape by the first of July.

New telephone lines stretched from Belton to park headquarters near the foot of Lake McDonald, around the lake and up McDonald Creek to its junction with Mineral Creek, then over the Continental Divide to St. Mary. Belton boasted a first class hotel with moderate rates, and the Great Northern Railroad's new "Swiss Chalets" were under construction. More tourist accommodations stood at the head of Lake McDonald.

Concerned as ever with conservation of the nation's natural resources, Grinnell supported efforts for two new national parks— one on the Olympic Peninsula and the other at the Grand Canyon— and pressed for a national forest in the Appalachian Mountains. After hearing that the Great Northern Railroad planned to build a road for automobiles from Midvale (East Glacier) to Lower St. Mary Lake, he decided to visit the new national park and see what was happening in the country he had long regarded as his "private estate. . . . Is there a trail out from Altyn up to my lake, which is on my glacier?" he asked Logan.

Somewhat dismayed by the developments already under way, he wished to see "Glacier National Park for the last time before it gets full of wagon roads and hotels." Elizabeth planned to go along to visit their Blackfeet friends, but Grinnell doubted his wife would go into the mountains, noting in a letter to Luther North: "her courage seems to fail her where the big hills cast their shadows." Still, he asked his mountain companion Jack Monroe to provide as much comfort in the camp as possible: "a cook, tents, reasonably good food, and generally someone to do the hard work."

The Force of Habit

The Grinnells launched their first "Glacier" experience at the Blackfeet Medicine Lodge on the Fourth of July. Blackfeet friend and storyteller Brocky, blind and gap-toothed, gave Elizabeth his walking stick. On a side trip to Belton they met Major Logan and studied a relief map of the park in his office, then rode in the rain with Dr. Charles B. Reed of Chicago to Avalanche Basin. "The Sperry Glacier was sometimes visible through clouds. It seems to lay on Gunsight Mt.," Grinnell wrote in his notebook.

Elizabeth stayed at Flower's boarding house in Midvale while her husband packed into Red Eagle Lake and up the St. Mary River with Joe Kipp and Henry Norris. Civilization had penetrated his wilderness: in camp he read a newspaper, noting the event in his diary with a hint of incredulity. A horse rolled over a cliff and fell over one hundred yards into the stream bed, saved from serious injury by landing on its packs; Elizabeth was no doubt happy she was not along.

Grinnell sold *Forest and Stream* to Charles Otis in the fall of 1911 so that he could devote more time to researching and writing a definitive study of the history and culture of the Cheyenne Indians. Jack Monroe advised his friend to travel abroad:

> Take a good rest, go and see how those old countries are (you have never blowed about seeing Europe around our campfires) and don't go to work until the Spirit calls Hard. I believe to drink a little whiskey to help break the old habit of Hard work would be wise, and help break the High Tension under which you have been living so long.

But old habits die hard. Over the next fifteen years Grinnell established himself as a leading historian and ethnologist through his four books on the Cheyenne: *The Fighting Cheyennes* (1915), *The Cheyenne Indians* (1923, in two volumes), *When Buffalo Ran* (1923) and *By Cheyenne Campfires* (1926). Elizabeth's photographs illustrated most of these. Grinnell also wrote numerous papers and several other books on Indian ethnology, plus a tribute to Frank and Luther North called *Two Great Scouts* (1928). In addition, he edited two volumes for the Boone and Crockett Club—*Hunting in High Altitudes* (1913) and *Hunting and Conservation* (1925).

Jack Monroe kept his friend abreast of changes at Glacier National Park, reporting in March 1912: "Jim Hill is building a number of hotels and camps . . . one lot of cabins at the foot of the Lake—one at the Narrows, and one at the second Narrows, and some at Gunsight Lake." Grinnell viewed these developments with ambiguity, replying, "I shall not greatly enjoy seeing them; but after all, that is what the Park is for—the benefit of the public." At times the public's enthusiasm for the park amused him: "I have already met one or two persons who described it to me and told me I ought to go see it!" he wrote Daniel Doody that spring. Even Grinnell realized personal benefit in the new accommodations, acknowledging to Luther North that after spending a few days packing the previous summer, he had become "too old for that sort of work."

The Grinnells met Luther North and his wife at Browning in August to share their 1912 vacation with these old friends. Grinnell rode horseback thirty miles along the automobile road under construction from the train station to St. Mary. He logged in his diary that he felt "Tired, stiff on arrival" at Jack Monroe's ranch. Two days later, as he and North rode toward East Flattop, they met three horsemen. Grinnell recorded:

> The leader spoke and at length asked if this was Mr. Grinnell's party and if I was Mr. G. Just before we turned off to McDermott, they stopped again and the leader introduced himself as Mr. Louis Hill [president of the Great Northern Railroad]. We had a long talk. . . . Hill seems a very bright, energetic and determined fellow. He will do much for the Park, and I told Jack he is a good man to tie up to. . . .

The party camped a mile below the falls at Swiftcurrent. Elizabeth decided to stay at the lakeside tent hotel while the others rode up to Iceberg Lake. Illness continued to haunt their excursions, but this time Elizabeth was not at fault: "Lute had one of his spells last night," Grinnell recorded on August 9, "and Mrs. North is sick. They will go to the railroad tomorrow morning." After their departure, the Grinnells, with Jack Monroe's children, climbed to Kootenai Lick to look for sheep.

> . . . Mabel and E. gave out half way up slope and Jesse staid behind with them. . . . Hattie and I went on and went to the top

of the ridge—Hattie climbed vigorously and went on ahead fast. I followed more slowly. From top of ridge we looked down into lick which extends for several hundred yds. along side of mts. coming out of sandy clay in shape of smelly salt springs . . . usually only a little dampness of soil. I tasted the water which had a distinct salty taste. . . . the mountains rise in abrupt cliffs . . . On SW face . . . there are bold vertical cliffs above and . . . another wide surface of broken rock, more or less level and without vegetation, where at some ancient date the whole side of the mt slipped away. . . . I recognized the place where I came with the Kootenais 27 years ago.

Before leaving the park Grinnell discussed the proposed dams on the St. Mary, Sherburne and McDermott (later Swiftcurrent) lakes with an engineer from the Bureau of Reclamation. Dam construction would require two million board feet of timber, prompting Grinnell to warn in his diary: ". . . Unless they log with discretion they may do much to mar the Park, which, according to this [the engineer's] story, is to be turned into a series of storage reservoirs and logging camps. Utilitarian Americans," he added sadly.

The Grinnells returned to Glacier Park the following year. "The force of habit keeps me still going to that dear place, though reasons for going there grow constantly fewer," he complained to Charles Reed in May 1913. A couple of weeks later in a letter to Edward Sawyer, he confessed, ". . . I continue to visit it even though it has been made a national park and is now more or less full of tourists." After a stay at the new hotel they traveled to St. Mary in only two hours by automobile, then camped at the head of Red Eagle and climbed toward the glacier. "The effort of climbing the hill and some carelessness about her eating, laid Mrs. Grinnell out," he related to Dr. Reed, "and before long we had to turn about and slide down, and took the automobile, if you please, for the big hotel."

Elizabeth spent the summer of 1914 in a cottage at Woodstock, Vermont, while her husband went to the Northern Cheyenne Reservation at Lame Deer, Montana. He skipped his customary visit to Glacier Park, where, he told Charles Reed, "you are pushed off the trail every few minutes by the multitude. . . ." The Great Northern Railroad, with its wholly owned Glacier Park Hotel Company, had hotels or camps at Glacier Park, Belton, Two Medicine Lake, Cut Bank River, the Narrows (Going-to-the-Sun) and the foot of St. Mary Lake and Gunsight Lake. The stone Sperry Chalet now stood complete, and another was under construction at Granite Park. A huge hotel had been started at Swiftcurrent to replace the Many Glacier camp, served now by a new wagon road from St. Mary. Autos, saddle horses or wagons could be rented at most sites; even motor launch service was available on St. Mary Lake and Lake McDonald.

In 1915 James Willard Schultz started a campaign to reassign Indian names to the park's geography, touching off a minor controversy with Grinnell, who objected for practical reasons: ". . . the white tourists cannot handle such names as Siksikakwan," he told Apikuni. "They have already dropped a syllable out of the mountain which I think is called Apistotoki and now call it Apistoki." Since the Blackfeet were Plains Indians, they "scarcely ever ventured into the mountains and identified by name only a few of the most prominent landmarks." Further, he believed some of the "old-timers" like Norris, Dawson, Kuteni Brown and Crow Quiver should be remembered, and he found Schultz's petition "comic but sad":

> Schultz, it seems, has the privilege of naming, or renaming, the mountains, lakes, peaks, etc., in the park. I have seen a partial list of the names, and they include those of his friends; old coffee coolers who used to lie around Ft. Benton or Ft. Conrad—regular scrubs—not one old time, respected chief in the bunch.

The petition, Grinnell told Schultz, "was signed by only nine people, of whom three or four were schoolboys and only one, Curly Bear, was a person of any particular standing." Robert Sterling Yard, of the new National Park Service, understood the problem and responded to Grinnell:

> A splendid front range in the Rocky Mountain National Park is named for a local prostitute. Others bear the names of farm hands and casual summer visitors. . . . Does James Willard Schultz deserve consideration? . . . They laugh at him in Glacier . . . everyone tells me he is a frightful drunkard. He writes a good letter and he has imagination—but that is the point; has he too much imagination?

The Grinnells took brief trips to Glacier during the summers of 1915, 1916 and 1917, staying most of the time in the comfort of the new Many Glacier Hotel. From this base they took short hikes up Canyon Creek, up Cataract Creek to Morning Eagle Falls, toward Iceberg Lake and into Apikuni Basin. Grinnell carried a pack containing their lunch, camera, sweaters and notebooks. "I am not accustomed to a pack," he told Jack Monroe, "and found it hard on my wind." On one outing he observed, rather wryly, "E. greatly tickled because a Mr. Adams to whom she spoke asked if she was Mr. Grinnell's daughter or his granddaughter."

Although pleased to see a trail to his glacier under construction during their 1917 visit, Grinnell's ambiguous feelings persisted, as he noted in a September letter to Edward Sawyer: ". . . the scenery was as beautiful as ever but the crowds there were larger than usual, and I became rather weary of the place after a time. . . ."

A Measure of the Man

Grinnell provided much of the information for Madison Grant's *Early History of Glacier National Park, Montana*, a pamphlet originally published by the National Park Service in 1919 and later included as a chapter in the Boone and Crockett book, *Hunting and Conservation*. In it Grant described Grinnell as representing

> . . . the now disappearing class of educated easterners who went to the frontier in the buffalo and Indian days and devoted their lives to the welfare of the great West. Many men . . . did the same, but . . . they were not unmindful of their own material interests, and the credit they deserve . . . is perhaps to be qualified somewhat by the fact that they . . . profited substantially. . . . Mr. Grinnell, on the other hand, from the year 1870 has freely given his time, his money, his scientific and literary attainments, and his talents to the cause of preservation of the forests, the wild life of the country and, above all, the welfare of the Indians of the West.

The idea for the park was "born in the brain of George Bird Grinnell," Grant wrote, outlining the visionary's leadership and guidance in its creation and acknowledging his role in naming many of the geographic features. Grinnell thought the references to him sounded like an obituary and lectured Grant on why he thought the general public would not be interested. In a January 1918 letter, he said:

> . . . if you are preparing a history of the Glacier national park which you expect to have appear in a Boone and Crockett book under my editorship, your labor is in vain. . . . You and I are like the rest of the public, in that we wish results accomplished. It is for that reason we struggle and sweat and fight for fifteen or twenty years or more, without apparently making any progress, and then of a sudden the things we were working for come to pass. We, ourselves, remember something of the time and energy and money expended to bring about the results but no one else knows of these efforts. . . . Moreover, no one else cares. People are interested in their own affairs, and most of them have little or no concern . . . for what may bring good to the public. Except for the few who think much about these matters, the question of what happened in Yellowstone Park forty years ago, or in Glacier Park twenty years ago possesses no possible interest.

The National Park Service printed the brief history unchanged, but the Boone and Crockett editor omitted many of the references to himself before the work appeared in book form.

Grinnell did not return to Glacier for three years. In the summer of 1920 he went alone. Elizabeth had been ill since Christmas, and though she was feeling better by summer, she remained in New York at a country hotel—Briarcliff—with a nurse. Her husband left, wondering in his diary "whether the mountains are still standing firmly on the other side of the St. Mary's Lakes." He stayed five weeks, riding the red hotel car between Glacier Park Hotel and Many Glacier, chatting with James Willard Schultz, who had arrived at the same time to write a book about the old days, and reminiscing with Jack Monroe. With Elizabeth absent, Grinnell told his sister, Helen, he was "absolutely without responsibility, and had a very delightful time."

Discord and Distinction

If his 1920 outing was delightful, the next year's trip was dismal. "The place was crowded so full of people that I got sick of it and moved off," he reported to Luther North. But crowds were not the real problem. After visiting Charlie and Nancy Russell at their Bullhead Lodge on Lake McDonald and discussing the automobile road proposed by the National Park Service to cross the Divide, the Grinnells returned by train to Glacier Park Hotel and then traveled on to Many Glacier. "Trouble to get a satisfactory room," he wrote in his diary on August 26, "overcharged for horse and had a squabble about horses with a new man who wished to give me a guide. I told him I would not have one." Irate, the Grinnells left, promising to write Stephen Mather, director of the National Park Service, and George W. Noffsinger, owner of the Park Saddle Horse Company.

In his letter to Mather the following April, Grinnell voiced several complaints. The hotel and saddle-horse monopolies exploited the public, especially the average man who had to spend wisely. Hotels were so expensive only the "well-to-do" could afford to use them. Renting a horse for $3.50 a day was exorbitant, allowing the concessionaire to recover the full cost of horse and saddle in but a few days. Hotel employees were discourteous, did not provide park information and discouraged walking tours while promoting the saddle-horse business. Still angry, Grinnell refrained for the moment from mentioning the issue of needing a guide.

He did not go to Montana in 1922; instead, he visited Luther North in Columbus, Nebraska. The next year he planned another stay in

Glacier, but not without advance preparations: "The last time I was there . . . I had so uncomfortable a time that I rather made up my mind I would not return," he explained to Arno B. Cammerer, acting director of the National Park Service. Though Grinnell recognized the helplessness of many tourists, a "wooden headed Park Ranger" had refused to allow him to rent a horse without a guide and showed him printed regulations to enforce the decision. He asked for a letter of exception from park Superintendent J. Ross Eakinand, stating, "Without such protection I do not care to go into the park."

Grinnell got Cammerer's letter immediately:

> Mr. Geo. Bird Grinnell . . . is one of the early explorers of the Yellowstone and Glacier National Parks. He knows both of these parks as well as he does his own backyard, and is to be afforded every facility of seeing Glacier Park. . . . The regulations requiring a registered guide to accompany his saddle horse party on the trails will not apply in his case. . . .

Someone passed the word. When the Grinnells arrived at Many Glacier Hotel in September they were greeted by its manager, the park ranger and the saddle horse concessionaire, all of whom obsequiously offered their services. After spending several days taking short trips, they struck out for Grinnell Glacier with two young men and a photographer who wanted to take pictures of ice caves. They followed the south side of Lake Josephine, crossed at its head, then rode up to the small spring where they stopped for lunch. They made the rest of the trip on foot. Grinnell noted in his diary:

> The trail was very steep in many places but the footing good. I had to stop rather often to get my wind. . . . E. and I went on toward the ice . . . reached and climbed the terminal moraine and sat down to await the others. Presently I went on under the lateral moraine . . . and found a small black cave. . . . I went back to E. who felt no disposition, as she said, to go further. I told her that she must at least stand on the glacier.

Slowly and carefully they walked up to the highest point on the ice. Halfway across, water trickled into a deep hollow peppered on its surface with potholes. "While on the glacier, we saw five goats. . . . On the way up saw a brood of golden eye duck . . . on the way down a water ouzel."

After several years of Elizabeth's coaxing, she and George finally toured Europe in the spring and summer of 1924. Even with this change of scenery, Grinnell felt isolated from Glacier Park, like a person visiting a house in which one once lived. "I knew . . . that if this was made a National Park that fact would mean my practical expulsion from the region," he wrote L. O. Vaught upon their return. Though he thought both Yellowstone and Glacier had been "ruined by the tourists," he saw good in their designation as national parks:

> If we had not succeeded in getting these regions set apart as National Parks, by this time they would have been . . . cut bare of timber, dotted with irrigation reservoirs, the game would have been all killed off, the country would have been burned over.

Elizabeth Grinnell joins her husband on Grinnell Glacier, 1923. —Glacier National Park archives

In 1925, in recognition of his efforts in conservation and for the promotion of outdoor life, Grinnell received the Theodore Roosevelt Distinguished Service Medal. As he stood in the East Room of the White House with two other recipients, conservationist Gifford Pinchot and teacher Martha Berry, President Calvin Coolidge remarked:

> Mr. Grinnell, I am struck by the fact that this year I have the pleasure of presenting these Roosevelt medals to three pioneers. You and Miss Berry and Governor Pinchot have all been trailblazers. In the case of Miss Berry and Mr. Pinchot, however, it is true only in a figurative sense.
>
> But you were with General Custer in the Black Hills and with Colonel Ludlow in the Yellowstone. You lived among the Indians; you became a member of the Blackfoot tribe. Your studies of their language and customs are authoritative. Few have done so much as you, none has done more to preserve vast areas of picturesque wilderness for the eyes of posterity in the simple majesty in which you and your fellow pioneers first beheld them.
>
> In Yellowstone you prevented the exploitation, and therefore the destruction, of the natural beauty. The Glacier National Park is peculiarly your monument.
>
> As editor for thirty-five years of a journal devoted to outdoor life, you have done a noteworthy service in bringing to the men and women of a hurried and harried age the relaxation and revitalization which come from contact with nature. I am glad to have a part in the public recognition which your self-effacing and effective life has won.[23]

Humble as ever, Grinnell told Luther North, "I went to Washington and with two other people stood up, listened to a speech by the President, and received the medal. . . . [It] is big enough to knock a man down with, and, I suppose, is actually something to be gratified about." When F. W. Whitehouse congratulated him, Grinnell replied, "It has seemed to me that the people awarding it must have made a mistake, but, after all, it is not for me to complain."

In late August 1925 he stopped briefly in Glacier after a trip to the West Coast. At Browning he saw Jack Monroe, Schultz and many old Blackfeet friends, and talked with Curly Bear about "various Piegan problems. It seems a shame that the P's have never been paid anything for the game and timber rights guaranteed them by the treaty of 1895 and taken from them when the park was established," he wrote in his diary. On his way out of the park he visited C. M. Russell and caught a glimpse of several unfinished paintings—one of a prospector discovering gold at Last Chance, another of Father

DeSmet addressing a great camp of Indians, and the last of an Indian riding up to a wounded cow buffalo. Russell died later that year.

In spite of his ambivalence about Glacier National Park, by 1926 Grinnell committed himself full time to conservation. He served on the American Game Protective Association's board of directors and as president of the National Parks Association and the Boone and Crockett Club. To his friends he wrote in words that now seem familiar:

> Most of us began as ardent hunters, but later our viewpoint changed.
>
> To look back on wild life as it was half a century ago is saddening, but the change of sentiment in recent years brings cheer. Many of us now recognize that we are trustees of this wild life for a coming generation.
>
> Within the term of the life of one man, species that formerly swarmed here in the wild state have disappeared. The natural inhabitants of the soil have been killed or crowded out, and man occupies the places where they once roamed, and fed and bred. Their homes are gone. We have cut down our forests, cleaned up our fields, drained our swamps and plowed up our lakebeds. Yet a new era has begun, and more and more people demand that refuges be set aside where the wild creatures may live and man may not encroach on them. This, as I see it, is the question of the day.[24]

Life Goes On

Although Grinnell did not realize it at the time, his journey to Glacier National Park that year and the climb to "his glacier" would be his last. He talked again with Jack Monroe and saw James Willard Schultz, who gave him a copy of his new book, *Signposts of Adventure*. "It has much good stuff in it ," he wrote in his diary that July, "but some mistakes." Elizabeth felt ill until they left for the East.

Tributes from the public arrived regularly at Grinnell's home on Stuyvesant Square on East Fifteenth Street. "Greetings to the Father of Glacier National Park," said the inscription below a snapshot of Grinnell Glacier. And on the accompanying card, "My 'Brownie' snapped this view while we hiked to Grinnell Glacier and I want to send it on to you as a slight token of appreciation for having founded this noble wonderland for us." Another thanked him for his effort in establishing the park and its "being a cure" for her grief after a death in the family.[25]

As he grew older and his world changed, Grinnell's excitement of life diminished. "With the passage of years," he observed in a

September letter to E. W. Sawyer, "the West has ceased to be wild and lost much of its attraction to me. . . . Most of the old Indians have passed on and the young fellows that have grown up do not know as much about Indian matters as I know, myself. In fact, they often come to see me for information."

Then, as he explained to Nonnie Lyon the following April, the excitement disappeared:

> Here in New York, life goes on in its usual commonplace way. Every two or three years I get out a new book, and my life seems to be devoted chiefly to keeping up a large correspondence and making a certain amount of copy for the printer.

The heart attack struck on July 14, 1929. He lay in his bed in grave condition for a month. "The doctor held out very little hope for recovery," Grinnell's secretary wrote Schultz, "but . . . he has surprised the doctors and is coming around in good shape." Weakened, he managed to walk a few steps to his chair, where he sat for hours, looking out at the big linden and oak trees in the park and down the street to the statue of Peter Stuyvesant.

He never regained his spirit and vigor. Three years later he wrote Jack Monroe: "So far as I can see there is no prospect of my ever getting out to Montana again." On Christmas Eve 1933, Jack tried to entice him West:

> We went over the St. Mary's Lake-McDonald Lake Auto Road last fall, and it is great. You can go in an auto, sleep in a feather bed, and live in a Steam Heated Room on most of our old campgrounds. Better come out and take a real pleasure trip and bid the scenes of our youth Good bye—

Grinnell stayed in his chair, looking out the windows of his study, until—except for James Willard Schultz, Apikuni, whom he said had "avoided most of the responsibilities of life," and Jack Monroe, "always up early and always ready to rustle stock"—he was the only one left. "Lonesome Charley" Reynolds had fallen in the Battle of the Little Big Horn. Billy Jackson died of tuberculosis on the last day of the century. Joe Kipp and old Brocky were gone, too, as were *Forest and Stream* business manager Edward Wilbur and editor Charles Reynolds. Hunting partner George Gould and "bully Teddy" had been long dead. And Lute, Luther North, had died three years before.

> . . . I see pass before me, as in a vision, the forms and faces of grave silent men, whom once I called my friends. They have fired their last shot, they have kindled their last campfire, they have gone over the Range, crossed the great Divide. There were giants

in those days, . . . how few are left alive! Lingering illness, the storms of winter, the pistol ball of the white man, the rifle shot of the savage, have sadly thinned their ranks. And none have risen, nor can arise, to fill places left vacant. The conditions which made these men what they were no longer exist.[26]

George Bird Grinnell died April 11, 1938, in his eighty-ninth year. The New York *Times* called him "the father of American conservation." The New York *Herald Tribune* said it better:

> The passing of Dr. Grinnell cuts a strong strand in the remnants of the thinning cable that still links America with the age of its frontier. . . . His happy and penetrating gifts as a naturalist gave George Bird Grinnell his peculiar foresight with reference to the fate of natural resources. . . . He could visualize and work toward the everlasting sanctuaries of the Yellowstone and Glacier National Parks. . . . His outstanding characteristic was that of never-failing dignity, which was doubtless parcel of all the rest. To meet his eye, feel his iron handclasp or hear his calm and thrifty words—even when he was a man in his ninth decade—was to conclude that here was the noblest Roman of them all.

We mold our heros in images to suit our needs; some soon disappear, replaced by others in popular memory. George Bird Grinnell strayed into obscurity, humble to the end.

Appendix A

Resolution of the Boone and Crockett Club, 1908

WHEREAS Senator Thomas H. Carter of Montana has introduced in the Senate a bill S. 5648, setting aside the Glacier National Park, within whose boundaries as fixed there is no agricultural or grazing land, nor any known paying mines or claims; and

WHEREAS the bill protects the rights of any and all settlers and bona fide miners in that region, does not infringe on the rights of any citizen or citizens, and will be a lasting benefit to the state of Montana, and to the United States at large; and

WHEREAS it is within the personal knowledge of many members of the Boone and Crockett Club that the proposed Park, lying within the main range of the Rocky Mountains, between the Great Northern Railway and the International boundary line is one of the most beautiful regions in the United States, comprising high rough mountain peaks and narrow valleys clothed with forests which, while commercially unimportant, protect its water supply; that among its summits lie some of the largest glaciers known in the Rocky Mountains from which flow important rivers, heads of the Saskatchewan, Missouri and the Flathead; that it is the region of many lakes; that it is from the abundant waters flowing from its mountains that a great area in northern Montana is proposed to be irrigated by means of the St. Mary's canal project and other irrigation projects, therefore be it

RESOLVED (1) that the Boone and Crockett Club record itself as heartily in favor of this measure, and urge the speedy passage of this bill, and (2) that a copy of these resolutions be sent by the secretary to the Honorable Thomas H. Carter.

—Glacier National Park Archives

Appendix B

Books by George Bird Grinnell

Pawnee Hero Stories and Folk Tales. New York: Charles Scribners & Sons, 1889.

Blackfoot Lodge Tales. New York: Charles Scribners & Sons, 1892.

American Big Game Hunting, ed. G. B. Grinnell and T. Roosevelt. New Haven: Yale University Press, 1893.

Hunting in Many Lands, ed. G. B. Grinnell and T. Roosevelt. New Haven: Yale University Press. 1895.

The Story of the Indian. New York: D. Appleton & Co., 1896.

Trail and Camp Fire, ed. G. B. Grinnell and T. Roosevelt. New Haven: Yale University Press, 1897.

Jack the Young Ranchman. New York: Frederick A. Stokes Co., 1899.

Jack Among the Indians. New York: Frederick A. Stokes Co., 1900.

American Duck Hunting. New York: Forest and Stream Publishing Co., 1901.

The Punishment of the Stingy. New York: Harper & Brothers, 1901.

Jack in the Rockies. New York: Frederick A. Stokes Co., 1904.

American Big Game in its Haunts, ed. G. B. Grinnell and T. Roosevelt. New Haven: Yale University Press, 1904.

Jack the Young Canoeman. New York: Frederick A. Stokes Co., 1906.

Jack the Young Trapper. New York: Frederick A. Stokes Co., 1907.

Jack the Young Explorer. New York: Frederick A. Stokes Co., 1908.

American Game Bird Shooting. New York: Forest and Stream Publishing Co., 1910.

111

Trails of the Pathfinders. New York: Charles Scribners & Sons, 1911.

Indians of Today. New York: Duffield & Co., 1911.

Beyond the Old Frontier. New York: Charles Scribners & Sons, 1913.

Jack the Young Cowboy. New York: Frederick A. Stokes Co., 1913.

Hunting in High Altitudes, ed. G. B. Grinnell and T. Roosevelt. New Haven: Yale University Press, 1913.

Blackfoot Indian Stories. New York: Charles Scribners & Sons, 1913.

The Wolf Hunters. New York: Charles Scribners & Sons, 1914.

The Fighting Cheyennes. New York: Charles Scribners & Sons, 1915.

When Buffalo Ran. New Haven: Yale University Press, 1923.

The Cheyenne Indians, 2 vol. New Haven: Yale University Press, 1923.

Hunting and Conservation, ed. G. B. Grinnell and Charles Sheldon. New Haven: Yale University Press, 1925.

By Cheyenne Campfires. New Haven: Yale University Press, 1926.

Two Great Scouts. Cleveland: A. H. Clark, 1928.

In addition, Grinnell wrote several pamphlets, including:

Social Organization of the Cheyenne, 1905.

Some Cheyenne Plant Medicines, 1905.

Brief History of the Boone and Crockett Club, 1910. Bent's Old Fort, 1923.

Audubon Park, 1927.

Grinnell also wrote numerous articles for *Forest and Stream*, a variety of magazines, and several natural history and ethnology journals.

Sources and Notes

Some readers have little concern about the authenticity of a book. For them, this section is placed at the back, out of their way.

A few readers would like verification, paragraph by paragraph. Copies of the master's thesis from which this book is derived may be found by these students at the Mansfield Library, University of Montana, Missoula or the Glacier National Park Archives, West Glacier, Montana. As a scholarly treatise presented for a post-graduate degree, the extent of annotation is almost excessive.

The remainder may find these notes both a comfort and a gratification to their curiosity.

Chapter I

Two sources provided most of the information for this chapter. The first, the Morton J. Elrod Collection, is held by the K. Ross Toole Archives of the Mansfield Library at the University of Montana, Missoula; Box 7, File 14 contains several papers and reports by Elrod that deal with Grinnell. In addition, the collection contains numerous photographs taken by Elrod over many years and several of his meetings with Grinnell that appear in this book. The other source is Grinnell's diary for 1926 in the Grinnell Collection of the Southwest Museum, Los Angeles, California. The collection contains his diaries and journals from 1870 to 1926 and a diverse group of materials that include letters to Grinnell, notes, manuscripts, and newspaper clippings.

1. This passage is from Grinnell's article, "To the Walled-In Lakes, IX, *Night in the Lodge*," published in *Forest and Stream* 26 (4 February 1886), 23. Like other contributors to *Forest and Stream*, Grinnell always wrote under a pseudonym; "Yo" is most common, and applicable in this case, although he also used "Ornis" on at least one other occasion.

Chapter II

A sixty-two page typed manuscript by George Bird Grinnell entitled "Memories" is the major source for this chapter. The manuscript, dated 26 November 1915, is an autobiography of Grinnell covering the period from his birth in 1849 to 1883, written "for the amusement of my nieces and nephews."

113

It ends abruptly in the middle of a word in the middle of a sentence. The copy used for this book is owned by University of Montana history professor Duane Hampton. A second copy of this manuscript, given to the Glacier Park Archives in 1956 by Elizabeth Grinnell, begins on mid-page twenty-four of the afore-mentioned copy. Finally, a manuscript that is identical to the first, but ninety-seven pages in length because of a difference in type spacing, was originally located at the Birdcraft Museum, Connecticut Audubon Society, Fairfield, and is now at Yale University, New haven. John J. Rieger used "Memories" as the major source of his book, *The Passing of the Great West: Selected Papers of George Bird Grinnell*, (New York: Winchester Press, 1972).

2. The quote "Though I had been West . . ." comes from a chronology compiled by Grinnell entitled "History of George B. Grinnell's Life." Three versions exists, each three pages in length with handwritten insertions. This quote is from the second version, as is the subsequent information about the meeting with Blaine and Custer. These papers were originally found at Birdcraft Museum, Connecticut Audubon Society, and are now at Yale University.

The entire George Bird Grinnell Collection at Yale University, New Haven, a major source for this book, is held on thirty-six reels of microfilm by the Mansfield Library, University of Montana, Missoula. The collection consists of thirty-eight letter books containing copies of Grinnell's outgoing correspondence from 2 August 1886 to 17 October 1929. Each book contains one thousand pages, the total representing about 31,000 letters. The collection includes also about one thousand incoming letters and a variety of correspondence and miscellanea.

3. Grinnell's description of shooting the antelope and breaking all four legs is from his "Memories." For details of the expedition, see Donald Jackson, *Custer's Gold: The United States Cavalry Expedition of 1874* (New Haven: Yale University Press, 1966).

4. Grinnell's letter about the destruction of western big game appears on page 61 of the War Department's *Report of a Reconnaissance from Carroll, Montana Territory, on the Upper Missouri to the Yellowstone National Park, and Return Made in the Summer of 1875 by William Ludlow*, Government Printing Office, 1876.

5. The delirium Grinnell describes in his "Memories" is difficult to identify; John F. Reiger suggests in *The Passing of the Great West: Selected Papers of George Bird Grinnell* (New York: Winchester Press, 1972) that Grinnell had Rocky Mountain spotted fever, but the illness occurred too late in the season and there is no mention of the typical and prominent rash that accompanies rickettsial infections. Colorado tick fever is also unlikely.

6. "We printed a good paper . . ." is quoted from a letter Grinnell wrote to Charles Sheldon, 11 March 1925; it and all other letters, unless otherwise noted, are preserved in the George Bird Grinnell Collection at Yale University.

7. Schultz's "Hunting in Montana" appeared in the 14 October 1880 issue of *Forest and Stream*. This article, "To Chief Mountain" and a number of other

James Willard Schultz writings are more easily found in a volume compiled and edited by Warren L. Hanna, *Recently Discovered Tales of Life Among the Indians* (Missoula: Mountain Press Publishing Company, 1988).

Chapter III

"To the Walled-In Lakes" (see Note 1) is the primary source for this chapter. Grinnell's description of his first trip to the St. Mary lake region appeared in fifteen weekly installments in *Forest and Stream* from December 1885 to March 1886. Some of the information is also noted in Grinnell's 1885 diary. He often used portions of his diary verbatim for his articles.

8. The description of Grinnell as he arrived in Fort Benton comes from James Willard Schultz's *Blackfeet and Buffalo: Memories of Life Among the Indians* (Norman: University of Oklahoma Press, 1962). Grinnell used the spelling "Appekunny" for many years before changing to the current "Apikuni."

The original "Four Persons" Blackfeet agency near Choteau on the Teton River was moved in 1876 to the "Old Agency," located on Badger Creek, a tributary of the South Fork of Two Medicine River, because the reservation boundary was moved by Executive Order in 1873 and 1874, leaving the original agency far to the south and off the diminishing Blackfeet lands.

9. They are hunting on Singleshot Mountain; their earlier hunts were on East Flattop.

10. The first four lakes now lie beneath Lake Sherburne, which was created by a dam just beyond the park boundary. The "great mountain with a triangular base" is Grinnell Point, for many years called Stark Point.

11. The three men had climbed along the southern slope of Altyn Peak. After Schultz returned to camp, Grinnell and Yellowfish climbed up Apikuni Creek to the lakes at its source, then across the saddle between Altyn Peak and Mount Henkel. Fine Shield Woman, Schultz's wife, had her hand crippled in the Baker Massacre in 1870.

12. Almost-a-Dog also survived the Baker Massacre. During the Starvation Winter, he kept count of the victims of starvation by cutting notches on a stick—555.

Chapter IV

Grinnell's announcement of the founding of the Audubon Society is in the 11 February, 1886 issue of *Forest and Stream*. Grinnell's diary for 1887 and an eighteen-installment series entitled "The Rock Climbers" in *Forest and Stream* from December 1887 through May 1888 are the main sources for this chapter.

13. James Willard Schultz took credit for naming Going-to-the-Sun Mountain and, since he was present, may have had a part in it. Joseph Kipp claimed the mountain was called "Pulls Down the Sun" but gave no hint as to this origin. Kootenai is now called Curley Bear.

14. The circular lake is now called Grinnell Lake, and another small lake north of the glacier is called Upper Grinnell Lake. These quotes are from part fourteen—*A River of Ice*—of "The Rock Climbers."

15. The letter containing the entry from Lieutenant Beacom's diary is preserved in the Glacier National Park Archives.

Chapter V

Details of the founding of the Boone and Crockett Club and the importance of sportsmen in conservation may be found in John F. Reiger's *American Sportsmen and the Origins of the Conservation* (New York: Winchester Press, 1975). Most of this chapter is derived from Grinnell's diaries, a series entitled "Slide Rock from Many Mountains," *Forest and Stream* 34 and 35 (6 March and 2 October 1890); a fifty-nine-page, three-part untitled manuscript that narrates the 1891 trip and a number of Blackfeet folk tales is in the Grinnell Collection at Yale University and the letter books. The block quote describing the fall of the pack horses is found in "The Crown of the Continent," *The Century Illustrated Monthly Magazine* 62 (September 1901).

16. William Jackson's grandfather, Hugh Monroe, was born at Three Rivers, Quebec, in 1799. Hired by the Hudson Bay Company in 1814, he was sent south from Edmonton House to the Sun River in Montana to trade with the Piegans. He was adopted by Rising Head, a powerful chief, given the name Rising Wolf, remained with the Blackfeet the rest of his life, and was the source of many of the folk tales preserved by Grinnell. The prominent mountain bordering Two Medicine Lake is named for him.

17. The "Colonel's Basin" was named for Robert Baring, who hunted there with his brother Thomas and James Willard Schultz in 1886; Grinnell listed the drainage as Baring Creek in his map notebook, 11 September 1891.

Chapter VI

A brief history of the mining activity in the Glacier Park region may be found in C. W. Buchholtz, *Man in Glacier* (West Glacier: Glacier Natural History Association, Inc., 1976). Letter-press books at the Browning, Montana, Museum of the Plains Indian are the source of the correspondence of the Blackfeet Indian agent. Most of the chapter is based on Senate Document 118, *An Agreement Made and Concluded September 26, 1895, with the Indians of the Blackfeet Reservation, Montana, by William C. Pollock, George Bird Grinnell, and Walter M. Clements, Commissioners Appointed under the Provisions Contained in the Indians Appropriation Act of March 2, 1895,* "Proceedings of the Council of the Commissioners Appointed to Negotiate with Blackfeet Indians," 54th Cong., 1st sess., 1896, Serial 3350. These "Proceedings" contain the actual statements of the participants and list all of the signers of the agreement.

A description of Altyn can be found in Muriel Sibell Wolfe, *Montana Pay Dirt* (Denver: Sage Books, 1963). Grinnell's diary for 1895 and the letter books in Yale's Grinnell Collection supplement the other sources.

Chapter VII

The letter books in the Grinnell Collection at Yale University for the years 1896 to 1906 are the main source for this chapter. Grinnell's diaries for 1901 and 1903 and an article, "Climbing Blackfoot," *Forest and Stream* 51 (8 October 1898) provided other material.

18. The letter to Gifford Pinchot, in the Yale Grinnell Collection, is dated 6 December 1901.

19. The article, "The Last of the Buffalo," appears in *Scribner's Magazine* 12, No. 3 (September 1892).

Chapter VIII

Again, the letter books in the Grinnell Collection at Yale University provide most of the information in this chapter. Studies on opposition to the park include an unpublished seminar paper by Michael Anderson, "Local Opposition to the Creation of Glacier National Park," located in the K. Ross Toole Archives of the Mansfield Library, University of Montana, and an article by H. Duane Hampton, "Opposition to National Parks," *Journal of Forest History* 25, No. 1 (January 1981).

Both of the bills Senator Thomas H. Carter introduced are titled *A Bill to Establish Glacier National Park*: the first was on 11 December 1907, 60th Cong., 1st sess., S. 2032, *Congressional Record* 42, no. 11, 269; the second was on 24 February 1908, 60th Cong., 1st sess., S. 5648, Congressional *Record* 42, no. 7, 6309. A useful but somewhat biased unpublished chronicle by Charles N. Pray, "Recollections Concerning the Establishment of Glacier National Park," dated 7 April 1954, is held by the Glacier National Park Archives; the K. Ross Toole Archives at the Mansfield Library, University of Montana, also has a copy.

Some of the historians who have addressed the role of the Great Northern Railroad in Glacier National Park legislation are; Donald H. Robinson, *Through the Years in Glacier National Park* ed. Raymond C. Bowers (West Glacier, MT: Glacier Natural History Association, 1960); James W. Sheire, *Glacier National Park: Historical Resource Study* (Washington, D.C.: U.S. Department of the Interior, National Park Service, Office of History and Historical Architecture, 1970); C. W. Buchholtz, *Man in Glacier* (West Glacier, MT: Glacier Natural History Association, 1976); and Madison Grant, *The Early History of Glacier National Park Montana* (Washington, D.C.: Government Printing Office, 1919). For a contrasting perspective, see David Walter, "Early Glacier-Area Developments, 1800-1910," unpublished manuscript (Missoula: University of Montana, Mansfield Library, K. Ross Toole Archives.

The Great Northern Railroad Collection at the Minnesota Historical Society, St. Paul, contains no evidence of an active role by the railroad in the establishment of the park.

20. The third bill Senator Thomas H. Carter introduced to Congress (26 June 1909) was also called *A Bill to Establish Glacier National Park*. 61st Cong., 2d sess., S. 2777. *Congressional Record* 44, no. 4, 3840.

117

21. The telegram to Hill is cited by Walter (see previous note). The three Republican senators it names were from states served by the Great Northern Railroad; Gilman, an assistant to Hill, worked in Washington, D.C., as a lobbyist.

22. The long-awaited piece of legislation that finally passed in the House on 13 April 1910 was *Glacier National Park*, 61st Cong., 2d sess., H.R. 767, *House Reports* 2 "Miscellaneous II," 5592. Grinnell's celebratory editorial is entitled "Glacier Park Bill Passes House," *Forest and Stream* 74 (23 April 1910).

Chapter IX

The letter books for 1911 and 1929, and other letters dated to 1933 in the Grinnell Collection at Yale University, are the principal sources for this chapter. The two articles by Madison Grant appear in "Early History of Glacier National Park," Department of Interior, National Park Service (Washington, D.C.: Government Printing Office, 1919) and "The Beginnings of Glacier National Park," *Hunting and Conservation* (New Haven: Yale University Press, 1925).

23. President Coolidge's comment to Grinnell appeared in the New York *Times*, 16 May 1925; see also, Albert Kendrick Fisher, "In Memoriam: George Bird Grinnell," *The Auk* 56 (January 1939).

24. Grinnell's letters advocating conservation went to J. H. Burnham, P. A. Tavener, H. Willard Reed, T. Gilbert Pearson, Robert M. Mitchell, Lee Miles, Hoyes Lloyd, E. Lee Le Compte, F. K. Vreeland, and Ray P. Holland, 4 February 1926.

25. The note and snapshot sent to Grinnell came from Inez L. Ponsche, 29 August 1927; the letter attesting to Glacier National Park's curative powers came from Lucy A. Sweeny, 4 September 1927.

26. Grinnell's comment about Apikuni came from a letter he wrote to Jack Monroe, 22 November 1928; the comment about Monroe is from a letter he wrote to George Gould, 9 November 1892. The block quote is from "Yo's" article, "To the Walled-In Lakes, IX. *Night in the Lodge*," *Forest and Stream* 26 (4 February 1886).

Bibliography

Bruce, Robert. *The Fighting Norths and Pawnee Scouts*. Lincoln: Nebraska State Historical Society, 1932.

Buchholtz, C. W. *Man in Glacier*. West Glacier, Montana: Glacier Natural History Association, 1976.

Farr, William E. *The Reservation Blackfeet, 1882-1945: A Photographic History of Cultural Survival*. Seattle: University of Washington Press, 1986.

Goetzman, William H. *Exploration and Empire: The Explorer and the Scientist in the Winning of the American West*. New York: W. W. Norton and Company, 1978.

Graham, W. A. *The Custer Myth: A Source Book of Custeriana*. Harrisburg, Pennsylvania: The Stackpole Company, 1953.

Grinnell, George Bird. *Pawnee Hero Stories and Folk Tales*. Lincoln: University of Nebraska Press, 1961.

_____. "Introduction." In *The Works of Theodore Roosevelt*. Vol. 1. New York: Scribner's, 1927. xiii-xxv.

Hanna, Warren L. *Stars Over Montana: Men Who Made Glacier National Park History*. West Glacier, Montana: Glacier Natural History Association, 1988.

Hodge, Frederick Webb. *Handbook of American Indians North of Mexico*. Vol. 2. New York: Rowman and Littlefield, Inc., 1965.

Holterman, Jack. *Place Names of Glacier / Waterton National Parks*. Helena, Montana: Falcon Press, 1985.

Jackson, Donald. *Custer's Gold: The United States Cavalry Expedition of 1874*. New Haven: Yale University Press, 1966.

Marx, Leo. *The Machine in the Garden*. Paperback reprint. London: Oxford University Press, 1968.

Morison, Elting E. *Turmoil and Tradition: A Study of the Life and Times of Henry L. Stimson*. Boston: Houghton Mifflin Company, 1960.

Morris, Edmund. *The Rise of Theodore Roosevelt.* New York: Ballantine Books, 1980.

North, Luther H. *Man of the Plains: Recollections of Luther North, 1856-1882.* Edited by Donald F. Danker. Lincoln: University of Nebraska Press, 1961.

Reiger, John J., ed. *The Passing of the Great West: Selected Papers of George Bird Grinnell.* New York: Winchester Press, 1972.

_____. *American Sportsmen and the Origins of Conservation.* New York: Winchester Press, 1975.

Robinson, Donald H. *Through the Years in Glacier National Park.* Edited by Raymond C. Bowers. West Glacier, Montana: Glacier Natural History Association, 1960.

Runte, Alfred. *National Parks: The American Experience.* Lincoln: University of Nebraska Press, 1979.

Schultz, James Willard. *Blackfeet and Buffalo: Memories of Life Among the Indians.* Norman: University of Oklahoma Press, 1962.

_____. *Recently Discovered Tales of Life Among the Indians.* Compiled and edited by Warren L. Hanna. Missoula, Montana: Mountain Press Publishing Company, 1988.

Wolle, Muriel Sibell. *Montana Pay Dirt.* Denver: Sage Books, 1963.

PAMPHLETS

General Information Regarding Glacier National Park, Season of 1914. U. S. Department of Interior, 1914.

Grant, Madison. *The Early History of Glacier National Park, Montana.* Washington, D.C.: Government Printing Office, 1919.

Grinnell, George Bird. *Audubon Park: The History of the Site of the Hispanic Society of America and Neighboring Institutions.* New York: Printed by the Trustees, 1927.

MAGAZINES AND JOURNALS

Barrett, Glen. "Stock Raising in the Shirley Basin." *Journal of the West* 14, No. 3 (July 1973).

Emmert, John W. "Pleasure Ground for the People." *The Naturalist* 9, No. 2 (1958).

Fisher, Albert K. "In Memoriam: George Bird Grinnell." *The Auk.* 56, No. 1. (January 1939).

Grant, Madison. "George Bird Grinnell." *The American Review of Reviews.* 71 (January-June 1925).

_____. "The Beginnings of Glacier National Park." *Hunting and Conservation*. Edited by George Bird Grinnell and Charles Sheldon. New Haven: Yale University Press, 1925.

Grinnell, George Bird. "Game Protection Fund." *Forest and Stream* 20 (May 5, 1884).

_____. "New Publications: Hunting Trips of a Ranchman." *Forest and Stream* 24 (July 2, 1885).

_____. "The Famine Winter." *Forest and Stream* 25 (October 16, 1885).

_____. "To the Walled-In Lakes." *Forest and Stream* 25 (December 10, 1885 to March 18, 1886).

_____. "Bird Destruction." *Forest and Stream* 25 (January 14, 1886).

_____. "The Audubon Society." *Forest and Stream* 26 (February 11, 1886).

_____. "Songs or Feathers." *Forest and Stream* 26 (March 11, 1886).

_____. "An Audubon Magazine." *Forest and Stream* 27 (January 13, 1887).

_____. "A Review." *The Audubon Magazine* 1 No. 1 (February 1887).

_____. "Membership of the Audubon Society." *The Audubon Magazine* 1 No. 1 (February 1887).

_____. "The Rock Climbers." *Forest and Stream* 29 (December 29, 1887 to January 19, 1888) and 30 (January 26 to May 3, 1888).

_____. "Slide Rock from Many Mountains." *Forest and Stream* 34 (March 6, 1890) and 35 (October 2, 1890).

_____. "The Last of the Buffalo." *Scribner's Magazine* 12 No. 3 (September 1892).

_____. "Charley Reynolds." *Forest and Stream* 47 (December 26, 1896).

_____. "Snap Shots." *Forest and Stream* 50 (April 23, 1898).

_____. "Climbing Blackfoot." *Forest and Stream* 51 (October 8, 1898).

_____. "Make Forest Preserves Game Preserves." *Forest and Stream* 56 (February 16, 1901).

_____. "The Crown of the Continent." *The Century Illustrated Monthly Magazine* 62 (September 1901).

_____. "The Appalachian National Park." *Forest and Stream* 57 (October 12, 1901).

_____. "The Forest Preserves as Game Preserves." *Forest and Stream* 57 (December 7, 1901).

_____. "Our Forest Reserves." *Forest and Stream* 58 (March 8, 1902).

_____. "More National Parks." *Forest and Stream* 65 (September 9, 1905).

_____. "More National Parks." *Forest and Stream* 65 (October 14, 1905).

121

_____. "Proposed Glacier National Park.-I." *Forest and Stream* 71 (December 12, 1908).

_____. "The Glacier National Park.-II." *Forest and Stream* 71 (December 26, 1908).

_____. "The Glacier National Park.III." *Forest and Stream* 72 (January 9, 1909).

_____. "The Glacier National Park.-IV." *Forest and Stream* 72 (January 25, 1909).

_____. "Glacier National Park." *Forest and Stream* 72 (February 20, 1909).

_____. "Glacier National Park." *Forest and Stream* 72 (April 10, 1909).

_____. "The Glacier National Park." *Forest and Stream* 74 (March 5, 1910).

_____. "Speak for the Glacier National Park." *Forest and Stream* 74 (March 19, 1910).

_____. "Glacier Park Bill Passes House." *Forest and Stream* 74 (April 23, 1910).

_____. "The Glacier National Park." *Forest and Stream* 74 (May 21, 1910).

_____. "The King of Mountains." *American Forests and Forest Life* 35 (August 1929).

Hampton, H. Duane. "Opposition to National Parks." *Journal of Forest History* 25 No. 1 (January 1981).

Mitchell, John G. "A Man Called Bird." *Audubon* 89 No. 2 (March 1987).

Olch, Peter D. "Treading the Elephant's Tail: Medical Problems on the Overland Trails." *Bulletin of the History of Medicine* 59 No. 2 (Summer 1985).

Runte, Alfred. "Pragmatic Alliance: Western Railroads and the National Parks." *National Parks and Conservation Magazine* 48 No. 4 (April 1974).

Schultz, James Willard (Apikuni). "To Chief Mountain." *Forest and Stream* 25 (December 3, 1885).

Stimson, Henry L. "The Ascent of Chief Mountain" in *Hunting in Many Lands*, ed. George Bird Grinnell and Theodore Roosevelt. (New York: Forest and Stream Publishing Company, 1895).

DOCUMENTS

Indians Appropriations Act of March 2. Statutes at Large. Vol. 28 (1895).

U.S. Congress. Senate. *An Agreement Made and Concluded September 26, 1895, with the Indians of the Blackfeet Reservation, Montana, by William C. Pollock, George Bird Grinnell and Walter M. Clements, Commissioners Appointed under Provisions Contained in the Indians Appropriation Act of March 2, 1895.* "Proceedings of Councils of the Commissioners Appointed to Negotiate with Blackfeet Indians." 54th Cong. 1st Sess., 1896. *S. Doc.* 118, 8, Serial 3350.

Agreement with the Indians of the Blackfeet Reservation in Montana. Statutes at Large, Vol. 29 (1896).

Proclamation No. Twenty-nine. *Statutes at Large*, Vol. 29 (1897).

U.S. Congress. Senate. *A Bill to Establish the Glacier National Park.* 60th Cong. 1st sess., S. 2032. *Congressional Record.* Vol. 42, no. 1. (December 11, 1907).

U.S. Congress. Senate. *A Bill to Establish the Glacier National Park.* 60th Congress. 1st sess., S. 5648. *Congressional Record* Vol. 42, no. 7. (February 24, 1908).

U.S. Congress. Senate. *A Bill to Establish the Glacier National Park.* 60th Cong. 1st sess. S.R. No. 580. *Senate Reports*, Serial 5219.

U.S. Congress. House. *Glacier National Park.* 60th Cong. 2d sess. H.R. 2100, *House Reports*, Vol. 1, Serial 5384.

U.S. Congress. Senate. *A Bill to Establish Glacier National Park.* 61st Cong. 2d sess. S. 2777. *Congressional Record*, Vol. 44, no. 4. (June 26, 1909).

U.S. Congress. House. *Glacier National Park.* 61st Cong. 2d sess. H.R. 767, *House Reports*, Vol. 2, "Miscellaneous II," Serial 5592.

U.S. Congress. Senate. *The Glacier National Park.* 61st Cong. 2d sess. S. 2777. *Congressional Record*, Vol. 45, no. 5 (April 14, 1910).

U.S. Congress. House. *Glacier National Park.* 61st Cong. 2d sess. S. 2777. *Congressional Record*, Vol. 45, no. 5 (April 26, 1910).

U.S. Congress. House. *Glacier National Park.* 61st Cong. 2d sess. H.R. 1142, *House Reports*, Vol. 3, Serial 5593.

P.L. 171. *An Act to Establish Glacier National Park. Statutes at Large.* Vol. 36, Part I (1910).

U.S. Department of Interior. National Park Service. *Glacier National Park: Historic Resource Study* by James W. Shiere. Office of History and Historic Architecture. Eastern Service Center. September 1973.

UNPUBLISHED MANUSCRIPTS

Anderson, Michael. "Local Opposition to the Creation of Glacier National Park." Seminar Paper, Department of History, University of Montana, Missoula, 1971 (?).

Ashby, Christopher S. "The Blackfeet Agreement of 1895 and Glacier National Park: A Case History." M.S. diss., University of Montana , 1985.

Grinnell, George Bird. "Memories." Copy in Grinnell Collection, Glacier National Park Archives, West Glacier, Montana; also held at K. Ross Toole Archives, Mansfield Library, University of Montana, Missoula.

_____. Untitled. Forty-one page manuscript dated August 2-10, 1928, describing 1891 visit to the St. Mary's Lake region and various Blackfeet Indian stories.

Pray, Charles N. "Recollections Concerning the Establishment of Glacier National Park," (April 7, 1954). Glacier National Park Archives , West Glacier, Montana; also held at K. Ross Toole Archives, Mansfield Library, University of Montana, Missoula.

Reiger, John F. "George Bird Grinnell and the Development of American Conservation, 1870-1901." Ph.D diss., Northwestern University , 1970.

Walter, David. "Early Glacier-Area Developments, 1800-1910." K. Ross Toole Archives, Mansfield Library, University of Montana, Missoula.

COLLECTIONS

Morton J. Elrod Papers, K. Ross Toole Archives, Mansfield Library, University of Montana, Missoula.

Great Northern Railway Company Papers, Part I, 1862-1922, Series C. President's Subject Files. "Settlement and Development. Establishment of the Glacier National Park and other National Park Matters." Microfilm reel. Mansfield Library, University of Montana, Missoula.

George Bird Grinnell Collection, formerly at Birdcraft Museum, Connecticut Audubon Society, now at Yale University, New Haven, Connecticut. Held on thirty-six microfilm reels at Mansfield Library, University of Montana, Missoula.

George Bird Grinnell Collection, Glacier National Park Archives, West Glacier, Montana.

George Bird Grinnell Collection, Southwest Museum, Los Angeles, California. Held on eight microfilm reels at Mansfield Library, University of Montana, Missoula.

Museum of the Plains Indians, Browning, Montana. Letter-Press Books, Correspondence of Agents of Blackfeet Indians.

Index

Ahern, Lt. George P., 50
Allen,
Cornelia, 58
Maj. R. A., 31
Allen Mountain, 3
Almost-a-Dog, 31, 50
Altyn, 76, 79, 97
American Game Protective
Association, 107
Apikuni, see Schultz, James
Willard
Apikuni Creek, 28
Apikuni Mountain, 3, 40, 51
Appalachian Mountain Club, 83,
85
Arikaras, 51
Audubon,
John James, 5
John Woodhouse, 5
Victor Gifford, 5
Audubon Park, 5
Audubon Society, 35
Avalanche Lake, 79

Babb, Cyrus, 87
Baker, Maj. Eugene M., 61
Banks, T. C., 15
Baring Creek, 55
Barney, Ashbel, 77
Beacom, Lt. John H., 39, 40, 43,
45
Bear Pipe, 31
Bear Pipe dance, 23, 30
Bear Woman, 30, 31

Belly River, 51
Belton, see West Glacier
Black Hills, 11
Blackfeet, 33
Blackfeet Medicine Lodge, 76, 81,
98
Blackfoot Glacier, 52, 55, 66, 76
Blackfoot Mountain, 76
Blaine, James G., 11
Boone and Crockett Club, 48, 90,
94, 95, 99, 102, 107
Boulder Creek, 57, 59
Brocky, 108
Brown, John George "Kootenay,"
37, 101
Browne, Lt. W. C., 59
Bull's Head Mine, 76
Bullhead Lake, 66
Bureau of Reclamation, 95, 100

Cammerer, Arno B., 104
Canadian Pacific Railroad, 36, 56,
87
Canyon Creek, 59, 76
Cartee, Ross, 66, 67
Carter, Senator Thomas H., 77,
84, 89, 90, 93, 94, 95
Cataract Creek, 40, 51, 66, 101
Cataract Mountain, 58
Century magazine, 59, 63, 77, 94
Cheyenne, 33, 51, 77, 98
Chief Mountain, 21, 30, 35, 67, 69,
81
Clements, Walter M., 65, 66, 70

Cleveland, Grover, 73, 75
Cody, Buffalo Bill, 9, 14
Conrad, Charles E., 62, 65, 70
Cooke, Capt. Lorenzo, 61, 64, 66
Coolidge, Calvin, 106
Cracker Lake, 59, 76
Cracker Mine, 76
"Crown of the Continent," 55, 77, 80
Curly Bear, 101, 106
Custer, Lt. Col. George A., 11, 13, 19

Dana, E. S., 12, 15
Distinguished Service Medal, 106
Divide Mountain, 37
Dixon, Senator Joseph, 91, 92, 94, 95

East Flattop Mountain, 21, 37,66
East Glacier, 97, 98
Elrod, Morton J., 1, 2

Fine Shield Woman, 28, 30
Fisher Cap, 32
Forest and Stream Publishing Company, 15
Forest and Stream, 11, 12, 13, 14, 15, 16, 33, 35, 36, 48, 55, 77, 83, 84, 90, 92, 95, 98
Fort Assinniboine, 59, 75, 76
Fort Belknap Reservation, 64, 70
Four Bears (Matotopa), 32, 50
Fusillade Mountain, 57, 79

Ghost Dance, 52
Glacier Park Hotel, 103
Goat Mountain, 24, 25, 37, 53
Going-to-the-Sun Mountain, 37
Golden Stairs, 24
Gould, George H., 35, 36, 37, 38, 39, 45, 49, 50, 57, 62, 75, 76, 80, 93, 108
Granite Park, 49
Grant,
    Lt. Fred D., 12
    Madison, 90, 102

Great Falls Tribune, 84, 89, 92
Great Northern Railroad, 94
Grinnell,
    Elizabeth Curtis Williams, 1, 2, 3, 80, 81, 83, 87, 93, 98, 103, 107
    Frank, 6
    Mort, 6, 14, 65, 66
    Thomas P., 5
Grinnell Glacier, 83, 104
Grinnell Lake, 40
Gunsight Pass, 5, 79

Hague, Arnold, 73
Hairy Cap, 79
Hallock, Charles, 13, 14
Hamilton, A. B., 65
Harriman Expedition, 77
Harvey, A. C., 91
Henkel, Joe Butch, 51, 63
Hill,
    James J., 63, 84, 99
    Louis W., 94, 95, 99

Iceberg Lake, 51, 99, 101
Indians Appropriations Act, 64

Jackson, William "Billy," 53, 55, 58, 63, 75, 108
Jackson Glacier, 55
Johnson, "Liver Eating," 12

Kalispell Bee, 89
Kalispell Inter Lake, 88, 92
Kalispell, Journal, 89
Kennedy Creek, 50, 51
King, Clarence, 45
Kintla Lake, 89
Kipp, Joseph, 16, 30, 35, 53, 65, 69, 70, 98, 108
Kootenai, 22, 23, 30
Kootenai Lick, 66, 99
Kootenai Mountain, 37
Kunhardt, C. P., 15

Lacey Act, 15
Lake Josephine, 1, 2, 25, 40, 104

Lake McDonald, 88, 97, 101, 103
Landon, E. H., 15
Landusky, 64
Lewis and Clark Forest Reserve,
    75
Little Bear Chief, 67
Little Chief, see North, Capt.
    Luther
Little Dog, 67, 68, 69
Little Plume, 68
Little Rocky Mountains, 64
Logan,
    Sidney M., 89
    William R., 97, 98
Ludlow, Colonel, 12

Mad Wolf, 68
Many Glacier Hotel, 1, 101, 104
Marsh, Othniel C., 8
Martin, Newell, 77
Mather,
    Fred, 15
    Stephen, 103
Matthes, Francois E., 80, 83, 85
McDonald Creek, 49
Merritt, Gen. Wesley, 59
Middle Calf, 68
Midvale, see East Glacier
Monroe, J. B. "Jack," 37, 38, 39,
    40, 43, 45, 49, 50, 51, 52, 44,
    63, 65, 66, 75, 76, 77, 98, 99,
    103, 106, 107, 108
Monroe Peak (Angel Wing), 50
Mount Allen, 58
Mount Cleveland, 75
Mount Gould, 3, 45, 50, 57, 66, 79
Mount Grinnell, 3, 43
Mount Henkel, 3
Mount Jackson, 75, 76, 79
Mount Merritt, 59
Mount Monroe, 3
Mount Norris, 58
Mount Reynolds, 57, 79
Mount Siyeh, 59
Mount Stimson, 79
Mount Wilbur, 3, 66, 76

Natahki, see Fine Shield Woman
National Park Service, 101, 102,
    103, 104
National Parks Association, 107
Noffsinger, George W., 103
Norris, Henry, 53, 57, 58, 59, 66,
    98, 101
North,
    Capt. Luther, 9, 11, 12, 16, 35,
        36, 49, 50, 55, 91, 98, 99, 103,
        106, 108
    Frank, 9, 14
Northern Cheyenne Reservation,
    87
Northern Pacific Railroad, 15, 17
Northwest Mounted Police, 37, 45

Old North Trail, 19
Otokomi, see Yellowfish
Otokomi Mountain, 37, 50

Panic of 1873, 11
Park Saddle Horse Company, 103
Pawnee, 10, 33, 51
Peabody Museum, 9, 11, 14
Piegan Mountain, 57
Pinchot, Gifford, 76, 79, 85, 106
Pollock, William C., 65, 66, 67, 68,
    69, 70
Power, Senator T. C., 62
Pray, Charles N., 91, 93, 95
Pumpelly Glacier, 76

Red Eagle, 30, 31, 50
Red Eagle Lake, 38
Red Eagle Mountain, 37
Reed,
    Charles B., 98
    William H., 14, 16
Reynolds, Charles B. (Charley),
    11, 12, 13, 15, 53, 55, 83, 108
Reynolds Creek, 75
Riess, Hans, 2,
Roosevelt, Theodore, 47, 81, 85,
    106, 108
Rose, Charles, 19

Rose Basin, 37
Russell,
  Charles M., 103, 106
  Nancy, 103

Satterthwaite, Franklin, 15
Schultz, James Willard, 16, 19,
  21, 22, 25, 26, 30, 31, 33, 35,
  37, 38, 39, 40, 42, 43, 45, 49,
  53, 58, 61, 75, 101, 103, 106,
  107, 108
Seward, William H. Jr., 53, 55, 56,
  58
Sheridan Gen. Philip H., 11
Shirley Basin, 16
Singleshot Mountain, 24, 25, 37,
  50
Siyeh Glacier, 59, 64
Smith, Hoke, 62, 63, 64
Southern Cheyenne Reservation,
  81
Sperry, Lyman, 79
Sperry Glacier, 49, 98
St. Mary, 79, 97
Standing Rock Reservation, 81
Starvation Winter, 21, 31, 33, 50
Steell, Maj. George, 52, 62, 65, 66,
  69, 70
Stimson, Henry L., 53, 55, 56, 57,
  58, 76
Sweet Grass Hills, 79

Swiftcurrent Creek, 51
Swiftcurrent Lake, 25
Swiftcurrent River, 25

Taft, William Howard, 95
Third bill, 92
True, F. M. 58

United States Bureau of Reclamation, 87

Vanderbilt, Commodore
  Cornelius, 9
Vaught, L. O., 105

West Glacier, 97
White Calf, 64, 67, 69
Whitefish *Pilot*, 89
Whitley, Josiah, 15
Whitney, F. J., 63, 77
Wilbur, Edward R., 14, 15, 83
Willis, Bailey, 80, 91

Yard, Robert Sterling, 101
Yellow Wolf, 68
Yellowfish (*Otokomi*), 19, 21, 22,
  23, 24, 25, 26, 29, 30
Yellowstone National Park, 13,
  15, 17, 35, 63, 89, 105
Yellowstone Park Improvement
  Company, 15

128